Scan,...

THE SPACE

WITHIN THE HEART

By the same author

The Space Within The Heart

AUBREY MENEN

McGRAW-HILL BOOK COMPANY

New York   St. Louis   San Francisco
Dusseldorf   Mexico   Panama   Toronto

CONTENTS

[v]

CONTENTS

THE SPACE

WITHIN THE HEART

Chapter 1

WHAT'S IT ALL

ABOUT, GOTTLIEB?

1.

It was Pope John XXIII who caused me to make up my mind to find out who I was.

I went to a semi-private audience. I stood about in a throne room for a while with twenty other persons, and then he came in, affable, all in white. He came opposite me. I knelt to kiss his ring. The Papal Chamberlain told him my name and what I did. The Pope looked at me with a frown.

"What is your nationality?"

"English," said the Papal Chamberlain, looking at a list.

"No, he's not," said the Pope.

"It says so here, Holy Father."

"He is *not* English," said John XXIII obdurately.

I was still kneeling. A thigh muscle began to ache. I made to rise. The Pontiff put one hand on my shoulder and kept me down. He ran a broad forefinger right round my jawbone.

"Look," he said to his assistant. "These bones aren't English. Nor these eyes." He touched my grey hair. "Nor this."

"No, Holiness," said the Chamberlain obediently.

"My son," said the Pope to me, "you are Indian, aren't you?"

I was about to reply "Partly," but then I reflected that one does not tell Popes they are partly correct.

"Yes, Holiness," I said.

I rose and as I rose I sighed. I had heard the discussion so many times before, all my life through. This time it was from a Pope. That, at least, was a change, but little more.

We spoke a few words to each other as is the custom on these occasions, and John XXIII left me. He gave me a glowing smile as he shook my hand. But I could see that it was not meeting me that made him happy: it was being right. That, since he was infallible, was as it should be.

Shortly afterwards my father, who was indeed an Indian, died in the fullness of years. My mother, who was Irish, soon followed him. When the last of the mourners at her funeral had gone, I sat alone in our family house in England, the country of my birth. I felt in need of something to do and I decided it would be appropriate to the day if I set about furnishing my own tomb.

2.

This is being constructed in Boston University by a patient and dedicated man whose name is Herman Gottlieb. He is gathering my manuscripts, my letters, photographs and personal objects and storing them up in the Library, believing that they will be of interest when I am well and truly dead. He has sent me a certificate with my name in beautiful calligraphy. This I have hung on my bedroom wall for I regard it as my headstone. But my birthdays continue to roll on. At each of them Gottlieb sends me greetings but, I imagine, with slightly raised eyebrows: and one day I must do something about it.

In the attic of my family home my parents had kept two large tin trunks which they had meant, when they found the time, to fill with my manuscripts and books and send them to Gottlieb. But they had never done it. So now I got up and began to take what I could find upstairs. I took down the two portraits of my mother and father which had hung on the wall since I was born, and put them in the trunks. I put in the manuscript of the little book I had written telling the story of their marriage. I put in many other things and then I was tired.

I sat on the lid of the trunk and looked out at the English winter evening. The house was very silent. I said to myself, "What's it all about, Gottlieb?" Then because the house was so quiet, I said it aloud.

"What's it all about?"

3.

I did not mean what was in the trunk. I knew what that was about. The puzzle was different. I wanted to know who was the person who had felt bored in front of a Pope who was talking about him. He had been there, inside me, all my conscious life, hidden away, listening to Pontiffs and people talking over his head. He was not in the tin boxes (Gottlieb could never collect him) but he held the key to everything in the boxes. He knew who I really was. I did not. My mother and father were gone. There was no one else in the world who was near and dear to me. It was time to go and find him.

I sold the house. I arranged to have the tin boxes sent to Gottlieb, and I retired to Rome where I had lived for many years.

In Rome I remembered Descartes. He had been suddenly struck by a question very similar to mine. He wanted to know if he really existed, and he saw at once that it was going to be a difficult thing to prove. He therefore shut himself up in a large Dutch stove, presumably (though he does not say) unlit, and emerged with the proposition "I think, therefore I am." This was very good, so good that Catherine the Great summoned him to Moscow where, having proved he existed, he caught a cold and died.

All the same, it was not good enough for me. "Thinking" was all very well. But I wanted to know who was the

"I." Without knowing that, Descartes' proposition is imperfect. He did not explore the question himself, perhaps because of the fatal cold, perhaps because he saw with his clear mind that the answer would probably be very upsetting to religious and moral people, for whose good opinion he had great respect. In fact, the answer, as I intend to show, is the most disturbing thing a religious and moral person can ever hear.

I looked around for the Roman equivalent of Descartes' Dutch stove. I found it, in the Thieves' Quarter. It lies in the centre of the old city. It is approached by a piazza in which there is a market. This piazza leads by the narrowest of roads to another piazza, all enclosed. On one side of this piazza is a house with an iron door which opens with a key. Behind this is a long corridor and then another door with another key. Again there is a corridor, in which halfway along is set a door, double locked, that would seem to lead to a room. But behind it is not a room but a sunlit courtyard, some fifteen feet square. On the far side of this is a final door and behind it a small apartment of two rooms. It had been inhabited, I knew, by a famous thief who very often had occasion to live alone and unobserved. It was empty now and I rented it, giving out that I wished for no callers and no questions.

I furnished this apartment with my books, which covered all the walls, a bed, a table, one chair and a cupboard for my clothes, of which I kept only those that were necessary to be decent in the streets. Each morning I would rise and walk through the two piazzas to a third, the Piazza Navona with its three fountains. Here I would drink a coffee, watch the fountains, and then return through the two piazzas, through the three doors, across the courtyard and into the apartment, locking the doors behind me. I would stay there until I was hungry, which often did not happen until midnight. I would eat, and then sleep. The nights were very quiet. Sometimes, but rarely, I would be woken by the sirens of police cars, chasing a thief into his lair. But, as I knew, they would not catch him, for he would be away over the roofs, and nobody would ever have seen him or know anything about him. So I would turn over and sleep again.

After two or three days spent in getting myself used to being quite alone, I began my investigation.

I took down the Upanishads from my shelves and began to read them. For readers who do not know what they are I should explain they are short books of philosophical speculation compiled in India about 500 B.C. Readers who *do* know what they are will already have turned to the end of this little book, confident that I found God.

I admit that would have been the respectable thing to do. The Upanishads are held in awe by many people in the West, a number of whom have had the satisfactory, not to say flattering, experience I have just mentioned. I did not. This may have been due to my Indian background. The Upanishads, though reverenced in the West, are really not much read in India. The average Indian prefers the Bhagavad-Gita, a beautiful poem in which the Lord Krishna teaches us the noble lesson that we must do our duty to society. The duty under Lord Krishna's atten-

[6]

tion in the Gita is to kill, maim or otherwise dispose of the enemy on a field of battle in a petty dynastic war. The Lord Krishna heartily recommends that this be done and done with a will. Indians, I have noted, have a liking for filling their minds with elevated notions which do not interfere with the business in hand. No book has ever been written which does this better than the Gita.

The Upanishads, on the other hand, teach no moral lesson whatever. The attitude in them is much like that of the Scottish philosopher David Hume. He wrote a book proving that there was no such thing as cause and effect. At the end of it he remarks that he has no doubt that his reasoning is correct, but as for himself, he has not the slightest intention of letting it affect him or his way of life. In the same way the philosophers of the Upanishads, after having led the reader into the very depths of his being, with shattering results to all his dearest beliefs, advise him to get up and go and enjoy himself like anybody else, with, they specify, horses, chariots, food and women. The verses in which this is said are as coarse as a hearty laugh and a slap on the back. How people manage to find God in such a book I cannot say, but I think it may be that they have a natural refinement which puts things decently straight.

The Upanishads are, in fact, a supreme monument to the fact that, in matters of religion, the Indians are eccentrics. From the earliest times, the Hindu faith was outlined in the Rig-Veda. This described the gods to be revered and how to worship them down to the last detail. For centuries they were believed to be the last word on the matter, but then some philosophers decided they were not. Having taken due thought, they came to the conclusion that the gods of the Rig-Veda were probably fictitious and that to worship them was quite unnecessary. In any decent and ordered society—that of the Christian Middle Ages, for instance—these daring men would have been promptly burned alive.

The Hindus, instead, studied these teachings, wrote them down, and then bound them up along with the Rig-Veda. It is hard to find a parallel to this act in any other religion. It is as though in each copy of the Jewish and Christian Bible, the Pentateuch was followed by some lively chapters saying that Yahweh did not exist, that the Temple was a highly redundant institution and that the Ten Commandments were binding on nobody but Moses, who had probably invented them for his own convenience.

Now the Western world is brought up to believe that black is black and white is white and anybody who attempts to muddle the two is an idiot. This opinion has carried us along a triumphal way of scientific discoveries which have culminated, for the time being (or forever), in the hydrogen bomb. The Hindu has never thought in this manner. He has always felt that anybody who could prove that black is not black, white is not white, but both are really the same thing, is a very clever fellow and worth listening to. The result is that the Indians have invented nothing at all, except some ideas. One of those ideas is that the only way of meeting violence is to do nothing about it, but to go on quietly minding your own peaceful affairs. I might observe in passing that if the bombs do go off, this will, obviously, be the only way of putting the world together again.

4.

I found the Upanishads dealt directly with my problem, but in a typically Hindu way. They begin by saying that the way to discover what it is all about is to find out who I really am. This much I had seen for myself.

But they go on to demonstrate that the way to find out who I am is to discover who I am not. As I have said, this sort of contradiction is much loved by Hindus, and the Upanishads grow downright whimsical in playing with it, sending earnest enquirers scampering away to look at themselves in pools of water in the forest and to come back in a hundred years.

I shall re-state the method for our less sunny times.

A mother has just put her three children to bed and is watching her husband as he sits in front of the television, dozing with his mouth open. Imagine that some ill-mannered visitor were now to ask "But after all, who *are* you, Mrs. Robinson? Don't answer. I will tell you. You are the harassed mother of three obstreperous children and the bored wife of a perennially tired husband." Supposing she has not enough energy left to slap the visitor's face, she might reply "You think so? Just give me one thousand dollars cash and a ticket to the Bahamas, and I'll show you who I am."

Now it is clear that this simple domestic scene contains an important truth. Not one of us believes that we are what the world has made us, and nothing else. We each put it in our own way. The middle-aged executive wonders what has happened to the little boy who used to go off fishing: he goes off fishing and does not find out. The professor puts down his Horace and wishes he had never left the family farm to go to college. The defeated general spends his days writing his memoirs to show he was never really beaten at all, and he believes every word he writes. The highly bred, sensitive, intellectual woman starts going to bed with the bell-hop because he is such a rough (as Thomas Mann so graphically describes in one of his novels). All these in their own way are discarding a *persona* that the world has made for them—and *of* them—in order to find somebody more truly themselves.

But at this point neither I nor Thomas Mann are really necessary. The reader will have started doing the thing for himself.

5.

As the Upanishads describe it, the process is like peeling an onion. One by one, you strip away those parts of your personality which consist of the things that you do because the world taught you to do them, or made you do them. Layer by layer—your parents' advice, your schooling, your job, your social position—all go. These are not you. Now it is the turn of your most intimate affairs, your secret hopes, your fears, your dreams. They, too, come from outside you, and they go. At last you come to your loves, your sexual life with others. You cling to those. Surely they are truly your own?

But they go. It took me nearly a month, sitting in my quiet room, to see that they had to be discarded, like all the rest. Later, I shall explain why and how. At this point, I must ask that the fact be taken on trust.

Then, one evening, after a long day of thought in which I did not leave my room even to eat, I saw that everything had gone and there was no more to discard. I looked for my true self.

Now if you peel an onion of all its layers, you find nothing. And that is exactly what I found.

I put away the Upanishads, for they had achieved their purpose. I had arrived at the very core of my being. The Upanishads, which are written in poetry, call it the space within the heart.

I was there. *I.* Not the person now weighing 72 kilograms and whom my mother and father had named Aubrey Clarence: not the writer of this book: not the person whose life, when he is dead, will be displayed in a glass case one day by Mr. Gottlieb (or so he promises me). Another person.

I gave it a name. I called it the Tranquil Eye. The play on words amused me, and it was near the truth. I found I could retreat into the space within the heart whenever I wished. For a time, I needed the quiet and loneliness of my room to do it. Later, when I gave up my room and returned to my normal life, I found that I could retreat into the space anywhere, even in company, for the sheer pleasure of doing it. The Tranquil Eye had seen an unforgettable sight. It had seen the whole of my life lying around it: and it was most comical. For it saw that my life had been the laborious construct of other people, some well-intentioned, some malign, some just interfering. It has been a life of emotion invented for me to feel. It has been a life designed so that I should never be my own man: nor would I ever have been had I not shut myself up in that room in the Piazza Farnese.

I have only to remember this, and I am the Tranquil Eye again, looking out like some objectively-minded goldfish from its bowl. But there is no goldfish and no bowl. There is, I must admit, no Tranquil Eye, for this is merely a device to describe things. There is only an empty space to be used as a post for observation.

There is, let me hasten to add, no ethereal blue light. There is, indeed, some sort of feeling, and it is much deeper than "I think, therefore I am." Sometimes I described it to myself as a sort of disembodied laughter, but in doing so I was merely a writer making a phrase about something which no phrase can describe.

6.

I must now narrate in detail the way I shed my enforced lives and what they were: but I shall do so in part. The biography of a writer should finish with his first success. From then on his life is spent with books and among books. He may go bare-chested, he may hunt big game, he may have a dozen love affairs (in between chapters) or, as in my case, he may go riding off into the deep Sahara on a camel. It is all the same. I have seen a picture of myself on a camel. I look exactly like a writer sitting on a camel.

But the fact remains that the only way of getting to the space within the heart is to go through the process of examining your false self. It cannot be attained by prayer, or by controlling your breath, or by taking a drug. It is as pure an intellectual process as learning a foreign language, and like that, it must be done by going over the same lesson again and again.

I have said that such a thing would be tedious to repeat if it were about myself, because of my profession. But there is another difficulty bound up with the argument itself. From the point of view of the space within the heart, the true Ego, the Tranquil Eye, has no patience with egoism. A king, a film star and a bum look very much alike to the surgeon who lays them open on an operating table. It is well known that the best way to stop thinking about yourself is to talk about yourself, and that is why so many people do it. The converse is also true. When you know yourself for what you are—or what the world has made of you—you prefer to shut up about it.

I would rather, then, describe the process in some abstract manner, but I have found it cannot be done. That part of the Upanishads which I experienced is not metaphysical: it is not a philosophy. It is the first experiment in history in psychological analysis. So I must present myself, and to alleviate that, I shall present portraits of people that I have known, in all parts of the world. I shall look at myself, and them, from the point of view of my room in Piazza Farnese.

Chapter 2

THE BOY WHO

WAS ALWAYS IN BED

1.

Even now, as I sit down to tell the story, the feeling that the space within the heart is a private place comes back to me and I have taken a turn or two about the room, reluctant to proceed. I think that I would have stayed locked within my discovery for many years, perhaps forever, if it had not been for a visitor. It was his problems which drew me out of my seclusion, for I found that I could see them with a greater clarity and understanding than I had ever had in my life. I could solve them, too, or go some way to helping him to a solution. He, then, is the true begetter of this book.

One afternoon while I was in my room I was disturbed by a knock on the door. Very unwillingly, I opened it and found Piero. He was a Roman boy, then about twenty, and a boy of exceptional beauty, set off by dark, knowing eyes. I had known him for some years, but he had disappeared, as these boys do.

He was holding a plate on which was a large bunch of bananas. When he saw me, he slowly knelt, put the plate at my feet, and then folded his hands in a derisive sketch of an Indian greeting.

"Master," he said, "I bring offerings, for I seek wisdom."

"Piero," I said, "get up and stop playing the fool. Where have you been since I last saw you?"

"Everywhere. And you? I hear you have become a *guru.*"

"Who told you that?"

"The porter."

"I bribed him to keep his mouth shut."

"Yes. But he said it didn't matter if he talked because you weren't a thief. Can I come in?"

"Of course."

He walked in, slim, not very tall, with a slow grace in his step. I noticed, as did everybody else who saw him, how beautiful he was.

That was his trouble. He had been born, like the poet Horace, in Venosa, deep in the south where the inhabitants were noted for their good looks and utter poverty. His family had migrated to Rome and became tenant farmers not far from Ostia. There, in spite of having fourteen children, eight of whom were surviving, the family made ends meet. In this they were helped by Piero, who, at the age of eight, broke into a wine-processing plant at night and stole a quantity of copper utensils, which he sold. In spite of the paradox, this might be called the last honest act of his life.

At nine he attracted the attention of the parish priest. He made it a habit to take young Piero on his knee and impart to him the elements of Christian morality. One day, to Piero's relief, he changed the subject and unbuttoned Piero's trousers. Piero watched the subsequent fumbling with awe, not for the priest, but for his brother, older by three years, who had predicted that this was exactly what the priest would do. Very soon Piero displayed an erection of considerable size, on which the priest said, "You're a naughty boy," presumably because he believed in the theological doctrine of Original Sin. After about twenty minutes the priest's conscience smote him. He hastily buttoned Piero's trousers and gave him some money. Young as he was (although nine is not very young in Italy), Piero recalls that he noted the marked difference between this money and the cash he had earned from the copper utensils. Then everyone called him a little thief. Now nobody could call him anything.

A day later the priest called on Piero's parents. He told them he had seen the makings of a priest in little Piero, and that, if they consented, he would pay the by no means light costs of sending him through the best seminary in the district. His motives are not clear, but probably he thought that, new priests being hard to come by, God would accept his sacrifice. Piero was thus offered up as a lamb, if not quite spotless.

The seminary gave Piero an exceptionally fine education. Nobody opened his trousers, and Piero, now fifteen, began to feel that indeed he had a vocation although he had come to it in a roundabout way. He felt, and still feels, he would like to be a priest. Then one day, while sorting out the laundry, another seminarian called Sandro flung himself on Piero and they made love among the baskets. The affair continued for several months until it was discovered. Piero was immediately blamed for seducing Sandro, because Piero was so beautiful, a verdict which had no logic in it at all. Sandro was sent to a stricter seminary. Piero was sent home.

The parish priest now had the mortification of being unabsolved in heaven and out of pocket here on earth. He gave Piero black looks whenever they met. But his sacrifice had not been altogether wasted. The seminary had taught Piero how to read books. Piero now began reading paperbacks which he persuaded his parents and his elder brother to buy for him. His favorite reading were books which explained in a particular fashion the teachings of psychoanalysis, partly because the subject matter was so different from the books he had read in the seminary. Trying to make friends again with the parish priest, he explained that the incident in the sacristy was not the priest's fault at all but was due to the fact that his mother had seduced him when young, but the priest gave him a sound box on the ear for his trouble.

Two years passed and Piero was more beautiful than ever. A woman ten years his senior fell in love with him while he was bathing. She took him to Rome; she took him to a tailor's. She dressed him. She took him to her apartment. She undressed him. Piero, at first shy at being

naked in front of a woman, decided that if he could not
be a priest, he had better be a man. He acquitted himself
well. The evening wore on into the night and the night
into morning. He acquitted himself as well the second
time, a little less well the third, and by the sixth time he
could not acquit himself at all. All the same, he had spent,
for him, a most interesting time, for he decided that he
was dealing with a nymphomaniac, the type of person to
whom whole chapters were devoted in his books. Besides,
he decided that being in bed with a woman was a lot better than love among the laundry baskets.

He went to live with her. His parents objected, but
Piero corrupted his mother. He gave her a television set
and then facilitated her fall. She got a washing machine, a
refrigerator, an unstainable carpet and many other things
that she had seen and desired. His young brother got a
motorcycle. But when his father asked for a small utility
car, Piero decided his constitution was not strong enough.
He decided on a change of life. Having read in his books
a great deal about the puritanism of England, he decided
to go there, for a rest. He ran away from his mistress, who
was frantic with grief.

His good looks were even more striking in England
than in Italy. He was received in English society with
open arms. Puritanism, he found, was no longer the fashion. He spent as much time in bed as before, but, this
time, not with the same person. In the intervals, he saw
some of the things he had read about—Buckingham Palace, the Changing of the Guard, the Houses of Parliament, and the English *gentleman,* a figure very popular

with the teachers in the seminary, who regarded him as a model of manners. He saw, in fact, three English gentlemen, all, once more, in bed.

He arrived at his eighteenth birthday without having done a stroke of work in his life, and with some money in a savings bank. He then met a girl from Chelsea, who upbraided him for his bourgeois life. She persuaded him to live the life of a rebel artist in her studio, and then to draw all his money from the bank for an abortion. Piero, penniless, returned to Italy and the family farm and quietly resumed his reading. This, in turn, led him to my room in the Piazza Farnese.

2.

Piero had come to learn from me, half jokingly, half in all seriousness, and I did my best. Let us examine his story, and in doing so, I shall demonstrate the first of the techniques I had discovered and used to distinguish my true self from my false selves. It is the transference in space and time to another frame of reference.

In Piero's case, let us transport him in our minds to the Arabian Nights. We know these stories as a book for children. In fact, the original Arabic version is a work in many volumes which gives a faithful picture of life in the time of Haroun-al-Rashid. It is so frank that it has only been translated fully twice, once into French and once into English. Neither translation is available to the general public.

Piero had been to bed with many women. In the time of Haroun-al-Rashid, everybody did. Monogamy and faithfulness in love would have been considered preposterous. A man kept as many women as he could afford. Passing from bed to bed at night was as commonplace a thing as putting out the cat is with us.

Piero had been to bed with men. In Bagdad a beautiful boy was an accepted object of desire, as, indeed, he still is in Muslim countries. It was a literary exercise to write poems to a boy's bottom, some of which are reproduced in the Arabian Nights.

Piero had been seduced at an early age. Transfer him once again to Imperial Rome. Once again we have some poetry, this time from Martial. He has many epigrams on the subject, in one of which he accuses a friend of making boys' pubic hair grow too quickly and causing their voices to break too soon. Transfer him once again to the Mermaid Tavern. More poetry. William Shakespeare is reciting from his favorite work, "Venus and Adonis." Venus, a mature woman, is attempting to have sex with Adonis. The age of Adonis is twelve, so she cannot.

Piero accepted money and gifts in exchange for going to bed. Take him back to the Arabian Nights. Beautiful boys were maintained by the rich, both men and women. They were given money and jewels. It was the accepted way of a poor boy laying the foundations of a career. With luck and skill in bed, a handsome lad could rise rapidly. Some even became viziers.

Other times, other customs, you may say, but if you do you will be missing a most striking corollary.

3.

We have seen that morals change with the times. If that is so, then when we make a moral judgement on a person we must do so from some fixed basis. That basis is always the assumption that the group of people we live among is the summit of creation.

To understand the proposition better, turn it inside out. Suppose that after due thought and much anguish we decide that the group we live among is not the summit of creation at all. On the contrary, people are too lazy to work, the country is bankrupt, crime is mounting and the politicians are too corrupt or too stupid to do anything about it.

We are then quite incapable of making a moral judgement until we can find another group which we can admire and say, "These people know the right way to behave"—the Catholics, the Russian Communists, for instance: or maybe we emigrate to another country.

This is exactly the situation that Piero found in England. He came there at a time when the English had lost part of their Empire, the country was living on borrowed money, and the politicians were despised. He found a swinging society, one, that is, that had lost its bearing and where, for the time being, anything went.

We never build our own morality because it cannot be done. In the eighteenth century, the philosopher Jeremy Bentham tried it and the strain drove him near to insanity. When he died his desks and bureaus were found to be filled with thousands of sheets of paper dividing everything under the sun into two. His skeleton was mounted and dressed for his trouble, and he now sits in a glass cage in University College, London, and nobody talks of the "greatest good for the greatest number" any more.

After his death, the moneyed middle classes of England decided that the way the moneyed middle classes of England behaved was the finest in the world, a belief much encouraged by the fact that about three-quarters of the world had become their property. This way of behaving was taught in special schools which were imitated everywhere. The result was the English gentlemen, whom Piero encountered in bed when they were, however, in somewhat reduced circumstances.

Part of this morality was (as everybody knows) derived from the Jews. The Jews were much more frank about the matter, for they declared boldly that they were the Chosen People. The early Christians who followed them improved on this by saying that they too were chosen, but chosen to be saved, while the others, including such Romans as Martial wrote about, would be damned. The French, from the time of Louis XIV, went the whole hog and declared that the only form of civilized behavior was to do what pleased the French. By the beginning of this century they had convinced the Western world, including Tsarist Russia, that this was true.

None of us escapes: whenever we judge a person to be a good man or a scoundrel we do so from the standpoint of the group we have accepted as ours, whether it be as small as our own caste or as large as a religion. If the person we are judging belongs to a group we do not know, we are at sea. We cannot tell if a Masai tribesman is a good fellow or not. If he cuts off the hands of a rival tribe and piles them in a triumphal heap, we can say it is not a thing we would do ourselves, but we are quite open to the suspicion that if we were Masai, we might.

It is just as bad when we judge ourselves. Every time we search our conscience, we are obliging our group with all the sweat and effort of a good soldier on the parade ground. We cannot call our faults our own: they are invented for us by parents and schoolmasters and the makers of the law. It may seem at first glance that if we lie abed in the morning we have the right to call it our own personal fault. We are lazy. But why are we lazy? Because we are not up and about doing things. Doing what? Plainly, it is only when we are doing absolutely nothing that we are free men. But you can do nothing in a most excellent fashion by lying in bed.

Piero brought me no more bananas after that first day. Instead we met each morning at the bar in Piazza Navona where I took my morning coffee. We sat at a table on the pavement, talking and looking at the fountains, undisturbed except by the occasional sighs of a Prince of the Byzantine Empire (or so he said); a tall, elegant man of sixty, who had, of course, fallen in love with Piero. Piero greeted him with Roman courtesy each morning —"*Buon giorno,* Your Highness. What news from Constantinople?"—and the poor man would blush and bury his head in his newspaper, for all the world as if he were trying to find out. For the rest, Piero snubbed him. He had more serious things on his mind.

One day Piero said to me, "I think there's something in what you say. There must be a Piero who is always Piero, whatever happens: the one in the heart of the onion." He paused. He drank off his coffee.

"I've found my father," he said. "I've been to see him."

For a long time Piero had known that the tenant farmer with whom his mother lived was not the man who begot him. In Italy, where there is no divorce, that is not an unusual state of affairs. No divorce means no re-marriage, but marriages break up just the same. Piero had several times asked who his real father was. But beyond telling Piero he was not a bastard—at which Piero was a little disappointed, for a bastard has romantic options open to him when he thinks of his descent—she would not tell him his father's name or what he did. If a document had to be signed for Piero, she would go off for two or three days and come back with the thing done, saying not a word. But when Piero was about to go to England, she had yielded. She had wept a little, taken him in her arms, and given him an address.

Piero told me this and fell silent. For a while we listened to the fountains.

"Where did you find him?" I asked.

"In jail."

"What for?"

"Shooting his mistress dead with a pistol. She had gone to bed with another man."

"How long did he get for it?"

"*Ergastolo.*"

It is the Italian word for a life sentence, and life in Italy means just that. His father might rot in jail until he died, unless, in his seventies, some president gave him an amnesty.

"The sun's getting hot," said Piero. "Let's walk over to the shade."

We sat in the shadow of one of the giant statues on the fountain. Piero dabbled his fingers in the water, like a child. But the expression in his dark eyes was that of a man, and a troubled one.

"What is he like?"

"Thin. Very pale. Dirty. The whole prison is filthy."

"How did you get on together?"

"There wasn't any of that wire screen you see in the movies," said Piero. "Just a room and a guard. My father stared at me. Then he burst into tears and hugged me. 'My son,' he said, 'my son.' "

Piero looked away. So did I. The Prince of Byzantium, scenting a quarrel, stared at us across the piazza.

Then I heard Piero laugh. He turned back to me and said, "My mother still likes him. She doesn't blame him at all."

"For having a mistress?"

"No. For shooting her. She says if he hadn't done it, she'd have shot the bitch herself. I daresay she would have. We've got hot blood, down there in Venosa."

"What do you think about it all, Piero?"

"About my father? Nothing much. He's a fool. Fancy

throwing your life away for a woman. There are so many of them."

"Probably not down there in Venosa. It's not Chelsea."

Piero smiled. "The old scoundrel asked me about the girls I knew. Fancy. After years in jail still thinking about women." Then he caught himself up. "Now *that's* a damned fool thing for me to say, isn't it?"

"Not really," I said. "When people go to prison for a long time you think of them as dead."

"Uh-huh," said Piero. "As a matter of fact, I don't think much about him at all. I think about myself."

"How?"

"In the way you said. Before I went down to that prison in Cozenza I was, well, me, Piero, the boy who was ready for a roll in the hay, up to a point, and don't ask me what point. But afterwards I was the son of a murderer."

"Does it make any difference?"

"Yes. Well, to me, no. Perhaps. I don't know. It makes a difference to other people. What do I say when they ask, 'Who's your father?' 'My father's a fine man but he's a permanent invalid'? That makes me a liar, and I'm not, really. Or do I say, 'My father's doing time for killing a whore'?"

"Have you ever told anybody but me?" I asked.

"Yes. A girl in London. I was in bed with her, of course. We'd made love. So she asked me and I told her right out."

"Was she shocked?"

"She said, 'Geeze' "—and Piero imitated the Cockney

accent very well. " 'Vi'lence. I'm crazy about vi'lence.' She opened her legs and said, 'Do it again, Piero, but be rough with me. Vi'lence,' she said, 'under the Southern sun.' Then she asked me if I was warm enough. They were *always* asking me if I was warm enough in England."

He got up. He thrust his hands into his trouser pockets. He kicked at a paving stone that was unevenly laid. "There's someone inside me who just sees it all going on, like you say," he said. "There's *got* to be."

He walked a step or two away, staring at the paving. Then the clock in St. Agnese in Agone began to strike. He looked up, smiled and said, "Come on. It's time you got back to your thinking. See you tomorrow."

4.

But the next day he was not there, nor the next, or the next. The Prince of the Byzantine Empire gave me significant looks over his newspaper, but beyond giving him a brief "Good day" and a bow of Byzantine stiffness, I ignored him. I drank my coffee and went back to my room.

On the fourth day, there was still no Piero. The Byzantine Prince was not reading his newspaper. He was, in fact, sitting on it, and staring at me with the expression of a dog begging a bone.

"Good morning," I said. "And what is the news from Constantinople?"

"Bad," said the Prince, shaking his head. "Your

young friend is on the Spanish Steps. He has joined the beatniks."

The Spanish Steps are a piece of architectural exuberance that all the world knows, and all the world photographs. For some time past, rebels from society from many countries had adopted it as their meeting place, to the intense annoyance of the police who were making a steady income clearing it for fashion photographers.

"He has grown a stubble and he is quite, quite filthy," said the Prince. Then, with a gush of words, he added, "And he was such a clean, handsome boy, too. How *can* he let himself go like that?"

He was clearly waiting for me to reply. I said, "His father's pretty dirty, too. Or so he told me." I got up, went inside to pay for my coffee and then went straight home.

5.

A week later Piero knocked at my door. He was indeed unwashed. It suited him, for it had removed the last trace of the seminary.

"Give me a cigarette," he said. "I've spent all night in jail."

I gave him one.

"Was it tough?"

"It stank of piss. Imagine: those cops *live* in it. They must like it, the bastards. They picked us all up on the suspicion of having drugs on us."

"Have you been charged?"

"No. Just clouted."

"You'd better not go back to the Steps for a bit," I said. "Next time while they're clouting you, they'll plant some weed in your pocket."

"Yes, Papa. But I'm not going back in any case. I've seen all I want to."

"What were the beatniks like?"

He sighed.

"They call it a pad, but it's still a bed." He laughed.

"Piero! Not another lover."

"Uh-huh. A Swedish girl. She said, 'Take me away from all this.' "

"Fun?"

Piero laughed again, very loudly, and bounced on my bed.

"I'd seen the movie and so had she," he said. "But seriously, she was a very intelligent girl. I talked about you. She helped me make up my mind."

He ran his fingernail against a shelf of books.

"Philosophy and all that are for *you*. It's not for *us*. You see, you're just running away from the facts, like all you older people. We have faced them. We know we're just animals, really. Top animals, I agree, but just a bundle of instincts. Sex mostly, like me and the Swede."

"Sex—and *aggression?*" I asked, for I knew he had been reading a fashionable book on the subject.

"A lot of that. You should have seen that cop's face when he hit me. Of course, there are writers like you and" —he paused—"painters like me."

[29]

I was surprised and showed it.

"Yes," he said carelessly, stubbing out his cigarette. "I've taken up painting a bit. I'm not bad. Naive. But you and me, we *sublimate*. That's all. But it's all instincts. So we live and die and that's all there is to it. Some of us are nice animals—and some animals are nice, aren't they?— and some of us nasty animals. So I've decided. Why should I stay here? I'm off. I want to go to some place where there are primitive people who just live as Nature meant them to. I can paint and make love and—wait, hold it—die of some foul disease, like Gauguin. What's it matter? Do you know of a place I could go?"

I did, because I had lived in one, years ago, when I had thought the same thoughts as Piero. But I did not tell him so just then. Instead, I took him off to a meal, in a small *trattoria* in the heart of the Thieves' Quarter. When they heard he had been hit by the cops they gave him a double helping of spaghetti, chicken and wine.

6.

When the meal was over we walked back to my room together. When Piero was inside, he patted the row of books he had treated with such contempt.

"I'm not really going to run away with that Swedish girl," he said. "I only said that to tease you."

He pulled out the volume of the Upanishads a little from the shelf, and then pushed it back.

"I'm finding myself, just as you say," he said. "I want

to go off for a while into the country and do some painting. And think."

"With the Swedish girl?"

He laughed with delight.

"You're jealous. No. I shall go alone. That's what you
said, wasn't it? You must be alone to do your thinking."

I nodded.

"Well," he said, *"arrivederci.* I'll be back one day
with offerings, O Master."

He winked, smiled, and was gone.

Chapter 3

THE DOLL

1.

I have just looked back on what I have written. I have just looked back at myself writing it—a skin on the onion, a writer bent over a blue sheet of notepaper with a yellow pencil in his hand, slipping into telling a lie as smoothly as the soft lead slides across the paper.

And such a soothing lie. Observe how easy I was making it seem. One takes a room, one reads a book, one sits and thinks, one finds peace, and peace is wonderful. Where was that skin of the onion aiming for, in his old age? California? An ashram maintained by rich old women looking for a lazy way to quiet their troubled souls. Indian things are sure to grow in popularity, and meditation sounds so lulling.

But *this* Indian thing I did was not lulling at all. I described one day of it, in a notebook I kept but which so far I have not opened. I shall now, and there it is. "Today was like a walk through Hell on an empty stomach."

2.

I must explain the empty stomach. I shall try to explain the walk, but that will be more difficult.

The Upanishads say that to think clearly you must free the mind from its appetites, for they tie it to the world about you. I had few such ties, and most were easily disposed of. Sex did not trouble me. I was not beset by gusts of passion. Sex torments few middle-aged men, though they torment sex in the hope that it will. I was not a boy, a sailor, or a roué. To be chaste was as easy as closing the door on a departing lover who has ceased to charm.

But eating was a profound nuisance. I was in Rome. The ancient Romans were very fond of food—there are whole menus in Horace. The modern Roman is even more fond of it. To him, a plate of *fettucini* and a chicken cooked with spices are poetry, art, music, and philosophy. For the latter, he cares nothing at all. But he lives to sit at table twice a day.

The waiters in the restaurants cosset him. They aim to have you rise from the table feeling that the world is a fine place and all's well. They have even more allure than a wife who is a good cook because they are too ignorant to have any conversation. But I had not shut myself up in my room to have cooks and waiters dictate my world view. I wanted to see things with clear eyes and that calls for an empty stomach, at least in this city.

So I took to eating the sandwiches that bars make, with disgust, for foreigners. I ate fruit as I read, or brought home a slice of plain cooked meat. I contracted my stomach when the edge was off my hunger. The human stomach, about which so much tedious stuff has been written, learns (I found) habits as quick and quicker than an intelligent puppy. Very soon my stomach contracted of its own accord. It still does, now that I am back in the world of waiters. I have had to teach them not to wring their hands when I leave food on my plate.

So much for that. "The doll," says my notebook. "You must face the doll."

3.

Gottlieb: In one of those two trunks you will have found two large pictures. One is of my father, the other my mother. They are photographs. They have been re-touched after the fashion of their time with such great enlargements. But there are other pictures, smaller, higgle-dy-piggledy in a boot box, and they show that the re-toucher had little to do to make my mother and father good-looking. My mother with her hair done in the fashion of King Edward the Seventh's mistresses, my father with his masher's quiff, make a handsome couple. In fact, at the time the pictures were made, my mother won a beauty competition.

These two portraits were always prominently displayed in any house that we lived in. They were our lares and penates, the household shrine. My father had the greatest contempt for all forms of religion. But he believed in God and prayed each morning, with a tiny leather notebook between his folded hands in which he had written some prayers of his own. He scratched the words "God is Love" on the frame of his own picture and said his prayers in front of it, each morning at nine o'clock. Throughout my boyhood I thought that he was praying to himself. When the hospital telephoned my mother to say that he had died in the night, she put down the instrument with a steady hand and in a voice that was just as steady she said, "There is no God." I think it may have been a bone of contention between them all their lives. There were many others.

But it had all begun wonderfully well. He had come to England to study to be a doctor; she had taken up nursing as an excuse to come to London from the country. They had fallen in love. They decided to marry. The year was 1910. The supremacy of the white races over the colored ones had never been so firmly established. My mother's announcement to her family that she meant to marry a black man quite spoiled the Delhi Durbar for them.

In the end, broadmindedness and the long view prevailed. England, as her subjects sang, held dominion over palm and pine. My father owned no pines, but he was heir to a very large number of coconut palms in far-off Malabar. He would thus, in a way, be bringing a bit of the British Empire into the family. My grandfather warned my mother that from his knowledge of Hindu law, she could not object if her intended husband took a second wife. My mother accepted the risk, and she married. My grandfather's knowledge of Hindu law did not extend to the fact that my father could be disinherited by the stroke of a pen for breaking his caste rules, and that was what happened as soon as the news of the nuptials reached India.

I do not know how many times my mother told me the story of this romance—my mother, never my father. Indeed, I never tired of hearing it. It was young love, with the daring of miscegenation to counteract the treacle. The part that I liked best in the narrative was where my white grandfather had stubbornly refused his permission for a whole day and my mother, in tears, had left to catch the train back to London. Then, when she was in the carriage and the train was ready to go, my grandfather had appeared on the platform, holding a great bunch of roses he had grown himself. He thrust them into my mother's arms, saying "Marry him, Alice, and God bless you, my little girl."

The scene sustained me through the trials of my boyhood, especially since my grandfather had told me it was all quite true. My parents were pioneers: I was the offspring of bold spirits who had opened the path to a new world where all the races of mankind could live in harmony together. It sustained me when English school companions called me the Rajah of Jampot and tripped me up so that I fell in the mud.

Forty years or so later my father came into his inheritance, when there was virtually nothing left to come into. He flew out to India to pick up the remnants. It was a new India, free at last from British rule, bubbling with excitement, especially among the young. They made much of my old father, whom they saw as a sort of prodigal son. They plied him with questions as to why he had left his native country to go and live among their ex-masters. My father found that he did not know, and then, again, he did know, and only too well. He fell in love with a girl of his own race, many years his junior. He wrote me strange letters, all aslant across the page, about her talents, her charm and how happy he was to be in this new, free land.

He returned to England. My mother and he came out to see me in Italy, where I had gone to live: they were grey-haired but still looking very much like the portraits in Gottlieb's box. In a hotel in Rome, while he stared out at the Aurelian Wall to avoid meeting my eyes, he said that he wanted to divorce my mother.

We went out and we walked in the Villa Borghese. I persuaded him to give up the idea. I thought then that I wanted to stop his world from falling apart. I see now that I wanted to stop mine.

4.

There was no divorce. My father saw that his love affair was an old man's folly. He settled down to life with my mother once again. He cultivated his garden. Voltaire had said that it was the remedy for all ills. But Voltaire was a very successful man. My father, as he pruned his bushes, began to see he was a failure. He wrote me a letter about nothing in particular, but which ended up, "Never be led astray by a woman's tears." So I suppose that before the touching scene on the railway platform, there had been other scenes less suitable for telling: walks by the river with my mother dabbing her eyes, and my father beside her, his mind in confusion under his straw boater, fearful of the step she was urging him to take, and even more fearful of never seeing her pretty, tear-stained face again. Once I had heard him say in company that there was a lot in favor of the Hindu way of choosing a bride for one's son whom he would not see until the marriage day. Everybody had laughed very much, except my father.

I saw him only once again, in Rome. When he returned to England, he wrote me a letter that was quite incoherent, spattered with phrases of Indian-English from his student days, phrases which I had never heard him use. My mother wrote, too, saying he had fallen strangely silent as they sat together in the evening.

One night he said: "Alice, my life has been a failure."

My mother protested that it wasn't so. She ran over a little litany of praise which she always kept handy: how he had done well on his own in the city of London, with few friends and an enemy on every corner; how they had lived comfortably for many years; how they had stood up to all the prejudice that surrounded them. And so on. When she told me all this, I saw in her eyes she had not understood in the heart what my father had meant.

I wonder now if he ever would have told her. I think not. He was a kind man, passionately fond of animals, and unwilling to cause pain to any living creature. The day after he had said he was a failure, he had a stroke, and was unable to speak. A month later he died, still in silence.

5.

I was with my mother for the first month of her widowhood. She talked a great deal about their marriage but she threw no light on it; or rather, she threw a golden glow on their years together, so it would seem they had passed like those long summer days we all remember in our childhood.

But once she said, a little sharply: "What were those letters your father wrote you?"

"Advice," I said. "A father to his son. You know."

She looked doubtful.

"Why did you never reply?"

We looked silently at each other for what seemed a long time.

"He would come down in the morning when he heard the postman," she said, when it was clear that I would not answer. "Then I would hear him saying, 'Why doesn't Aubrey answer? Why doesn't he *answer?*' "

She changed the subject. She grew nostalgic. Once more, for the hundredth time, I heard the story of my grandfather, the platform, the flowers and "God bless you, my little girl."

But suddenly one night I heard something else. I had taken her out to dine. Things had gone well. She was a little high when we got home, but we decided to have a final glass of champagne. I was glad to hear her laughing again.

She looked at the pictures on the wall.

"Do you know," she said, "why I married Kali?" That was his name. It was clear that she had gone right back into the past, before he ever became my father.

"No. Tell me."

"When I was a little girl," she said, "we used to dress dolls to give to the missionaries. I always chose a *brown* doll. I mean one with a brown face. Most of them were white: pink and white. But for me, no. I *had* to have a brown one."

She sipped her glass, her grey eyes dancing with amusement.

"So when I saw Kali in the hospital, looking so frightened and *so* handsome, I just said, 'That's the man I'm going to marry.' "

She became aware again that I was there.

"Your poor father," she said laughing. "He hadn't a chance. I bowled him over. I won a beauty competition, you know. You wouldn't think so to look at me now, would you? *Would* you?"

"You're still as beautiful as ever you were, Mother."

"Am I?" She ran her fingers over her cheekbone. "Well, I won't be in the morning if I stay up any later," she said. She rose. She gave me a long embrace and a kiss and went, a little unsteadily, up the stairs to bed.

I sat until four in the morning, staring at those pictures that you found in the box, Gottlieb, and finishing the bottle of champagne. Then I went to bed, and fell into a black and dreamless sleep.

6.

On the first day of my retreat to my room in Piazza Farnese I went for a walk. It was evening and I made towards the Tiber. I came to a bridge and halted. Before me lay the vast pile of Hadrian's Tomb, and the dome of St. Peter's, all against the setting sun, in one stupendous panorama. The tomb was dark against the sky.

It was on just such an evening that my father had spoken for the last time to me as his son. He knew he was going to die and he had come to Rome, which he had always loved. He had asked to be taken to see the tablet which has been placed over the niche where once was the urn with the Emperor's ashes, but he had been too tired to enter the building. So we had stood just where I was standing now, in silence.

"Animula blandula," my father had said, and then nothing more for a while. They were the first two words of the poem that Hadrian himself had written. They are addressed to his own trembling little spirit as it leaves his body as he dies, and he wonders where it is going, what it will do, so lonely, and with no one to comfort it. From my father's boyhood in faraway Malabar, it had been a poem that had meant a great deal to him. I can hear him now, reciting it to me, when I too was a boy, understanding

[41]

nothing but the sadness which it always brought into my father's voice.

The words, now, as we stood on the bridge, ran through my head.

My father had turned away. "Let us go home," he said. "It is beginning to get cold."

On the way back his spirits rose, as they always did among the Roman people, for they looked at him with the bold, admiring Roman glance. He had kept his good looks and he was a handsome old man.

In the bustle of the market in Campo de' Fiori he suddenly laughed.

"You know, if you were a good, Hindu son, when I was dead and burned, you would take my ashes and walk round my pyre, scattering them to the four points of the compass. Every Indian father wants that, even a damned skeptic like I am."

"In that case," I said, "I'll certainly . . ."

He threw back his head and laughed again, his silver hair floating away from his head. *"Bello,"* said a market woman, and smiled at him.

"I won't be burned on a pyre," my father said. "I shall be put away in a London crematorium by Mr. Killick. You don't know Mr. Killick, do you? Ah, but you will, my son, you will. He won't let you scatter my ashes: it's so un-British. But he'll sell you a memorial rose tree. Ten guineas."

We turned into a great piazza shadowed by a church.

"I wonder . . ." said my father, but did not go on. And then a little later:

[42]

"If I'd had the time . . . But, of course, I've had all the time in the world."

"For what, Father?"

"Reading. When I married your mother, I turned my back on my youth. I thought *my* father a backward fool and I despised the books he used to read. But when he died, I brought them back to England. Philosophy, religion, the Upanishads, the epics. When I grew old I began to read them, but it annoyed your mother. She would say, 'Why don't you take the dog for a walk?' So I did. Poor Peter! How he loved his walks."

And then at the door of my apartment: "You should look into the Upanishads. I'd like you to. They're difficult. Too difficult for an old brain like mine. But you're a writer. You'll be able to ferret things out. Don't give up too easily. There's something there. A great deal there. Come, let's hurry. Your mother will be fretting. We've been gone a long while."

Now he was gone forever. I left the place on the bridge where we had stood together. I went back to Piazza Farnese. I went through the doors, closing them behind me. I took down the Upanishads. I hoped my father was pleased, under his English rose.

7.

When my father died it all turned out very much as he had said. I met Mr. Killick. He was a tall, thin man in his thirties, dressed in black but wearing remarkably skittish shoes with long pointed toes, fashionable among the swinging young. He was not at all mournful. He was adept at making pithy comments and he liked to show off his skill. Thus when the arrangements for cremating my father had been made, I said, fatuously I admit, that I hoped everything would go smoothly.

"It hardly ever does," he said cheerfully enough, and in the event he was right. We lost my father's oldest Indian friend who was following us in his own car because our driver took a wholly unexpected turning, and the old friend never managed to find the crematorium.

"The driver's dodging a traffic jam," said Mr. Killick from the front seat of the black limousine. "Mustn't be late."

We were exactly on time: the tape-recorded organ started the moment my mother put her foot across the threshold (an electronic eye, I suspected). The elevator under my father's coffin worked to perfection, and he disappeared from my sight as gently as he had lived.

We went outside to look at the flowers. A light rain was falling on a stretch of concrete, a sort of parking lot which Mr. Killick supplied for the flowers.

"My father once mentioned that he would like me to scatter his ashes after the Indian fashion. Can that be done?"

"They'll be hot," said Mr. Killick, shaking his head. "And for quite a long time."

And he sold me a rose tree. Ten guineas. If I did not scatter my father's ashes, at least I took his advice and read the Upanishads. I am glad I did. I see now that he was trying to save something from the wreck of his life.

Chapter 4

THE EGG CELL

1.

For some time in my room in the Piazza Farnese I did not remember the doll. As we know from St. Anthony, any hermit is beset with temptations. Mine was to tell pretty lies. When you begin to examine yourself to find your true self, you dwell for a long time on the comforting myths that have got you by. Nor do you know they are myths. But one day, as you grow wearier and wearier to the heart of your being, you lose them. You see yourself naked and no lie will comfort you any more.

2.

I suppose, throughout my life, I have been reminded of my parents as often as an heir to a throne. It is a burden. Ralph Elliston, the Negro writer, once came to my apartment in Rome. He felt, as the book on my shelves behind him proclaimed, that he was an invisible man because of his color. Nobody looked at him. But in my apartment he was as visible as the electric light, which, if anything, he outshone. Women sat around his feet to look at him and had to be stepped over. Writing a book had in no way helped him to be treated like anybody else. Still less had it helped him to be treated like himself.

I have learned that for that to happen, you must first know yourself. Paradoxically, when you do, you do not give a damn about how people treat you.

When I was in my early twenties and a student at University College in London, I won a bursary called the "Rosa Morison" for an essay. I was overjoyed, and so was my father, for it was in the middle of the Depression and he was fast running out of money. I was given a parchment and some presentation volumes on some excuse, but I was regretfully told by the Dean that I could not have the cash. This was reserved for a student of "pure British descent on both sides." The Dean was academically indignant: to soften the blow he added that I at least had the advantage of being a member of two cultures and that could prove to be a great thing. Since his name was Solomon and he was a Jew, he should have known better, and probably did.

Nevertheless, the thought remained with me, whether walking the streets because I had no money to do anything else, or eating twopenny pies made of horseflesh. (Come to think of it, when I began training my stomach not to eat in Piazza Farnese it must have felt that it had been there before.) I wrote a play. It was called "Genesis 2" and ostensibly was a re-telling of the first few chapters of the Bible, but slowly turned into a tract about the oppression of one race by another. It began with a dialogue between God and a fertilized egg cell, and went on through Adam and Eve and Moses and Pharaoh's daughter, ending up (I now marvel how) on an Indian tea plantation. The play was presented to select audiences on Sunday evenings at the Fortune Theatre. The lead was played by a rising young star, André Van Gyseghem, who gathered a talented company around him. The Lord Chamberlain refused a license but that did not matter, since the audience was made members of a legal fiction called a club.

The play was well received on the first Sunday night. The critics (those who came) did not fail to mention God and the egg cell and the tea plantation. A few days later an enraged Lord Chamberlain rang up the owner of the theatre and told him to close the show on pain of having his license revoked. He hurriedly complied.

In due course I was summoned to appear before a magistrate at the famous court on Bow Street. Van Gyseghem filled the public seats with actresses and actors and directors with liberal views. A man with big black boots, called Mr. Titmus, testified that he, a police agent, had gained admission to the presentation (he had been given a free ticket to the gallery, which was empty). There he had witnessed a spectacle which according to his view was blasphemous and obscene. My lawyer looked immensely pleased, since, as he had told me, he was most anxious that the true subject of the play should not be brought up in court. He knew the magistrate; he was no churchgoer, but he was a staunch upholder of the British Empire. My lawyer pleaded my youth. He asked that my career should not be ruined, a most silly defense since every man jack in the court knew it would be the making of it. The magistrate asked if I had any money, to which I replied I had not a penny. He then rather inconsequentially fined me five pounds. Van Gyseghem passed his hat around the public benches and he soon had double the sum.

Reading the next morning's newspapers, I said to Van Gyseghem I could see why Mr. Titmus called the play blasphemous but not why he had said it was obscene. There was not—I am speaking of many years ago—a dirty line in the whole script. Van Gyseghem thought a while and said, "It was the egg cell in Act One. You see, it was fertilized, and Mr. Titmus knows just how that has to be done."

But among the cognoscenti I was launched on my career—not as an obscene playwright but as a fighter for the freedom of Indians on tea plantations and an anti-imperialist.

3.

When I came to examine this part of my life in my room in Piazza Farnese, I found it, at first, quite satisfactory. Solomon seemed right. I could stand between two cultures. I had pointed out the faults of one of them. Surely I could claim this to be at least part of my true self. I went to bed happy.

THE SPACE WITHIN THE HEART

I woke at five. Heavy rain was falling in the little courtyard. I stayed in bed, feeling too lazy to think. I idly picked up the notebook beside my bed. I saw the entry about the doll. I dozed a little and then jumped out of bed, fully awake and furious: just plainly furious, like any man in the street and not at all like a man meditating on the Upanishads.

Myself, my "Genesis," was the product of a little country girl playing with a brown doll.

"Neither English nor Indian, Holy Father. I am the child of a doll and a willful woman. May I ask your apostolic blessing for the doll, Holy Father? It was a very Christian doll. It was meant for missionaries, but I do not know if they were Catholic."

I said the absurd words aloud, but they did nothing to abate the tumult of my feelings. I strode up and down the narrow room, barking my shins against the bookcases. At last I could bear it no longer. I dressed and threw a raincoat over my shoulders. I went out, cursing the doors when they would not open easily. The rain beat against the vast façade of the Farnese Palace, making it drip like a grotto. The two fountains in the square tossed their spouts of water about, as though trying to trap the arrows of the rainstorm. Wet already, I walked quickly through the Campo de' Fiori, where the market women, huddled under sacks like witches, were setting up their stalls, shouting vulgar Roman jokes at each other in shrill voices to keep up their spirits.

I walked on till I came to the bridge where my father had stood. The dome of St. Peter's was a ghostly grey shadow. The great angel on top of Hadrian's Tomb was black and menacing, its huge wings pointing to a sullen, oppressive sky. The Tiber was yellow and green, like bile. I cursed the Upanishads.

What were they, after all, but a product of the doll? Why was I sitting in my room reading this Oriental mystification if it was not because of the doll? Who was the middle-aged man, his grey hair plastered to his head with wet? Who was he? Ask the doll. Titmus was right. The fertilizing of that egg cell had been an obscene affair.

I walked under the plane trees along the embankment till I could turn off and go to the Piazza Navona. Its vast harmony seemed to lighten the rainstorm and make it a stage effect for some baroque pageant. I went to the bar. The coffee was not yet ready in the urn. The aged bartender shook his head.

"Piove!" he said. *"Governo ladro."*

("Just look at the rain! What a government!")

The centuries-old Italian joke lit up a light in my mind, a golden, uncertain glow. I was in Rome. The coffee was ready. I drank it. I was in Rome. I went outside and stared at the piazza. The rain was stopping. *I was in Rome.* What that meant to me, just then I could not say. But I knew it was something to do with the doll: an answer for it, perhaps. I went back to my room, resolved to find out.

4.

I was greatly surprised by the depth of my own reaction, but as my solitary days lengthened I began to understand that these periods of bitter reflection were necessary stages towards the discovery of myself. Most of the thinking we do about ourselves is cosy and sentimental, like a tale by a woman novelist that we pick up to while away an evening by the fireside. Even if we go to a psychoanalyst to do our thinking for us, it is no better. We immediately find in him the friend we have been seeking all our lives. He in turn has been trained, not to say hardened, to expect this. He accepts the burden and thinks of his fee.

Then, when I had sat in front of the two portraits with my bottle of champagne, the brown doll had hovered in my mind in a luminous cloud of tender memories—my mother when young, holidays together, illnesses in which she had tended me. She was (perhaps I should have said this before) a good mother, and I thought about her as good mothers expect to be thought about by their sons. When she was alive I did not treat her as an object of logical and scientific analysis. But now she was dead I was assiduously botanizing on her grave.

I am, of course, doing that now. But I am doing it with calm. I shall not leap up from this desk and dash out into the streets of Rome. The calm, however, came only with long experience. My father once told me that he was glad he had given up his studies to be a doctor. He had, of course, no money to carry them on. But he told me that he could not bear to see women suffer. But had he continued, he would have learned to bear it very well, and if the woman was suffering in an entirely novel way, he would even have found it fascinating. It is the same when one begins to study oneself and the people who have affected one's life, not with hazy human-kindness, but with the neutral precision of a surgeon. Still, the first incision in one's first operation is a disturbing experience.

To recover from it, I made up my mind to spend a day reading. Since I wanted to rest from emotions, I turned to the shelves where I kept my books on science. I took down a volume on genetics. Great progress had been made since the days when I made my fertilized egg-cell talk with God. Piero had discovered that his father was a murderer; I had discovered my doll. But very soon there would be people who would discover that they owed one half of their genes to a totally unknown man masturbating into a hospital test tube. Looking only a little further ahead, there would be people who would discover that their quiet, orderly and friendly disposition was due to the addition of a molecule of this and a molecule of that to their genes, on the instructions of a computer with the very best of intentions towards society.

Such persons, I felt, would have a far more urgent need to find their true selves even than myself. So next day I took up my investigations again.

5.

The question that I took up was this: why had the thought that I was in Rome lifted my depression and calmed me? It had been a strange moment. I had felt very much like a child who has woken from a nightmare to find his familiar curtains blowing at his bedroom window. But why?

THE SPACE WITHIN THE HEART

When the sun was shining again, I walked to the temple of Mars Ultor and stayed there for over two hours. It is the ruin in Rome to which I go most frequently, because almost nobody else does. It is vast; it is magnificent; its columns are the finest in the city, but its entrance needs an effort to find and tourists rarely make it. Beside the podium of the temple are the remains of a marble meeting hall. On the ground is the outline of a huge foot; a colossal statue of an emperor once stood here; which emperor we cannot be sure, but few men have left behind them such a bizarre mark in history.

The podium is high and full of sudden hollows and broken stones. But at the risk of a twisted ankle I always clamber over it until I reach the three great columns that are still standing, almost as perfect as when they were first put up. Above them is a stretch of ceiling made of great blocks of stone, marvelously well-carved. Behind, shutting one off from the world, is a wall, higher even than the temple, which was built to hide the slums of the Subura. It is a very good place in which to think.

Gibbon sat on the wide steps of the Ara Coeli and looked in his mind's eye at the decline and fall of an empire. I sat in my columned nook and, more modest, looked into myself.

I remembered a holiday. I was a schoolboy, thirteen or fourteen perhaps, and overcome by the loneliness of that strange age. The fun of the beaches had gone grey and thin for me, my parents had become two importunate strangers who would not let me be. I felt, with each passing day, that more and more I was doing things and saying things that were not mine at all. I was laughing and shouting because others laughed and shouted. I was happy because on a holiday it was required of me. It was the mood in which boys in stories run away to sea. I ran away into the dim ages of pre-history.

I found an old and coverless guide to the island (I was on the Isle of Wight) written years ago by some Victorian clergyman with a taste for archeology. It spoke of barrows and mounds under which chieftains had been buried and pits to be found among the hollows of the hills where Bronze Age people had huddled in villages. An extraordinary sense of joy took hold of me. I went out and bought a large map, the biggest scale I could find, and opened it, rather tremblingly. There, sure enough, were the barrows, the graves, the tumuli, all marked and labeled in gothic type to show they were antiquities.

The next day, soon after sunrise, I was out among the hills, food for a day in a knapsack, the map carefully folded down at the part where the barrows were. I had to climb the side of a steep down to reach the first of them, or so the map said. But I could see nothing as I craned my head upwards. For a while I was in a panic that I had misread the wriggling contour lines. I checked, and climbed further.

Then I saw it, sitting high on the shoulder of the down, looking out to sea, low and long like a stranded whale, sublimely alone. I remember that I said to myself, "They must have buried Ulysses like this, on some lonely headland in Ithaca."

I climbed the barrow. I peered down into the pit

where they had dug and found a skeleton with iron brace-
lets. I sat down and looked at the sea and the rolling
green hills all around me. I could not see a single house. I
was by myself, out of the time of the world around me
and wandering in another.

From that day until the holiday ended I was among
the hills, finding the tumuli, tracing the villages, walking
along down-side paths that had been made before history.
I was very happy.

Sitting now under the colonnade in Rome, I could
see why. I had found something entirely my own. I never
told my parents about it; for years I never told anyone. I
would have liked to have told the Victorian clergyman,
had he not been dead and buried in his own churchyard.
But then, he would not have tried to steal it from me.

It is a passion which has remained with me all my
life: a passion, but even more a refuge. It has led me into
the Indian jungle, to finger the scattered heads of statues
lying among the creepers. It has led me into the Libyan
Desert and the innumerable pillars of Leptis Magna; to
the Dead Sea, and the oven-hot hill of Masada; to the
streets of Pompeii. When I was forty I settled down in a
house in Amalfi, not, as I told people, because it was a de-
lectable spot on an Italian Riviera, but because it was
near Pompeii. Whenever the world got too much for me
and people too demanding, I could go to this empty city.
I went so often that I know every street and alley in it. I
have seen it on a bitter January morning, under snow,
and totally deserted. I do not know that I have ever seen
anything so much after my own private heart.

6.

Returning to my room I made my second discovery. My first had been the peeling of the onion as an essential preliminary to getting to the true core of one's being. This second was that the space within the heart has a sort of antechamber, an approach which is locked with keys, very like my room on Piazza Farnese.

With myself it was my absorption with the remote past. With another person it could be one of a hundred other things. But whatever it is, it must be private. It must not be anything one was told to do by others. It must be yours alone, and done by you alone. To be short, the worst disaster I can imagine would be for me to have a wife who was interested in archeology. If she were bored to exasperation with it, that would be fine.

The locks of this antechamber should be well oiled, ready to click shut against the intruder, and they come in many guises. Thus, although I now know a good deal about archeology, I take care to know too little to go to conferences. Nor have I any ambition to dig. Archeologists on a dig are as sociable as Boy Scouts. I have none of their expectation of one day making a great discovery, like the tomb of Tutankhamen, a dream which keeps a great number of archeologists going, to say nothing of their fund-raising. Some time ago some of them announced that they had discovered the site of the legendary island of Atlantis. Much emotion was generated in the hearts of lovers of the past, except mine. I went to see the dig and found they had unearthed one commonplace Minoan house and some nondescript walls. The rest was fantasy, just as I had expected. I found it a most enjoyable trip.

That is why I have chosen Rome as a place to live. Provided I avoid foreigners, I can go among my ruins and never say or hear a word about them. The Romans have no love for their monuments and never have had any. One half of their masterpieces were made by ruthlessly despoiling the other half. Nobody can tear down a monument now—they bring in too much money. But if a true Roman ever mentions, say, the Arch of Constantine, it is to say that it is a risk to the circulation of traffic. They never go to see their ruins; they would be dismayed if I took them to see some fresh discovery—all of which pleases me very much. Sometimes, indeed, from good manners and hospitality, I will take a favored visitor from abroad to see some beautiful thing he might have missed; but only if I feel quite sure that he will be like those praiseworthy men of Cortez who stood silent on their peak in Darien.

One has to be very careful. Once, when motoring in the countryside between the city and the sea, I came across twelve great Roman altars, all in a row. They had just been unearthed. A forgotten spade lay up against one of them. The rough tin shelters that had been hastily put up made them look even more fresh to the eye. Nobody at all was about, except a peasant cultivating a distant field. For want of something to say at a party, I foolishly mentioned this. My luck was out. I had hit upon an enthusiast. He immediately organized an expedition—date, time, number of cars, where we would eat lunch, with a little note in his little book to read up the passage in Virgil which may or may not refer to the place. I never went on the expedition. I have never gone back to my twelve altars.

I am aware—I am stressing—the social absurdity of my point of view. But I need it, and, maybe, there are many people like me. One evening in Manhattan, where there is no archeology to be done, I went out and bought a child's box of building blocks. I made a fine ruin on the dressing table of my hotel room, so very interesting that I forgot I was due at a Broadway musical show. Why, I wonder, do people make so much fuss about being alone in a modern city? It is a valuable art: as valuable as having a cloak of invisibility in a concentration camp, because it serves much the same purpose.

As I found in my room, the road to the peace of the space within the heart is not straight and it is not easy. It is beset with storms of emotion such as mine when I went out into the rain. The solitude, the concentration, make the pictures in the mind vivid and harsh, like the colors of some once mellow masterpiece that has been cleaned by the restorers. They are pictures in which you see details that have, all your life, been comfortably hidden under the grime and the varnish. You have a sense of shock, as when, turning over the papers of some dead friend, you find a letter in which he says what he really thought of you. Later, after much practice, you learn how to deal with these moments; later, that is, when you have discovered your real self and can call it up to bring you calm.

But until then, to have some personal thing in which you can take temporary refuge, even if it is only some long fantasy you have made up all by yourself, is a very necessary safeguard.

Chapter 5

THE COLD EMBRACE

1.

"Walking too much on the Palatine Hill," said Henry James, "is not good for the soul." It was very good for mine: it helped me find I had one that I could call my own. Each day I left my room for an hour or so. I wound my way through the old Ghetto and so to the hill on which the Caesars built their palaces. I went no longer to the temple of Mars Ultor because that had served its purpose. I chose instead the northeastern slope of the Palatine, precipitous in places, and covered in bushes. Here are the great grey blocks of the temple of Cybele, the Mother Goddess who was worshipped by eunuch priests, and below, a scatter of random ruins where you may perhaps see one other person in the course of the whole day.

It amused me to sit awhile by the temple. The ancient Romans had imported the stone from where the Mother Goddess lived with great pomp because it was a fine piece of loot. Nothing showed that they were top dogs

better than this: other conquerors had robbed their vic-
tims of the gold; the Romans stole their very gods.

But after a while they drove the faith out of the city.
The behavior of the eunuch priests was even more scan-
dalous than that of the painted male whores who regularly
paraded on the Etruscan way, down below the hill in the
Forum. Then, at the height of the imperial age, they
brought the religion back again. The people liked it, and
it kept their minds off politics. Mothers are preoccupying,
whether they are of flesh or stone. Mine certainly was. She
wanted me to be her lover.

2.

I first became aware that my mother had carnal
thoughts about me when I was about sixteen. At that age
my mind was lively enough but as for my body, I gangled
with the best and my face had an unfinished look, as
though it had just been unwrapped from damp rags by a
sculptor who was not feeling at his best. I was not attractive to anybody, except my mother.

Seventeen years, as everybody knows, is a long time to
be married to the same man, especially when a woman
finds that the onset of middle age has done no great havoc
to her looks. My mother began to cast around for an ad-
venture. She became exceedingly hospitable to visiting Indians, particularly students. I chanced upon her one day
sitting on the knee of one of these, a handsome dandy. I
was not upset. I held very advanced views about sex; in

fact, I held very advanced views about everything. But I imagined that my father would be furious.

In due course, it seemed to me that he was. I heard raised voices in their bedroom; doors were slammed; pregnant silences became the order of the day at meals. A fine quarrel was raging, I knew, but it always stopped when I came in the door.

Now just at this juncture I had seen myself, for the first time, in print. A daily newspaper with a national circulation was seeking a student to brighten up its literary page. A romantic piece of pseudo-historical nonsense came their way in the shape of a book of biographies of highwaymen called "Stand and Deliver." They hit upon the idea of having it reviewed by a schoolboy. My English master having written for them, they asked him to choose the boy and he chose me. I wrote an enormously overlength review in which I said that highwaymen were blackguards and scoundrels who richly deserved hanging (though, as I recall it, I did not hold with capital punishment at the time). I also conveyed that the authoress of the book was a ninny.

The review was published in full; the authoress was asked to reply. She wrote a rather flustered piece, and letters followed. An editor rang me from the newspaper, said they were having fun in the office, and would I give them my views on the celebration of Armistice Day, the English equivalent of Memorial Day, but at that time used to glorify the First World War on the excuse of mourning the fallen. I obliged, with a similar success.

It was while I was working on this piece in my bedroom that I decided to have a showdown with my father. I went to him and said that I was doing some vitally important writing, and I could not get on with it in this atmosphere of tension. He heard me in complete silence. I took the plunge and, in my advanced way, said that if the quarrel was about the handsome dandy, he should have it out with him and forbid him the house.

At this point my father broke his silence. I remember being taken aback that such a slightly built and short man could produce such a bellow.

"Will you kindly shut your stupid swollen head and go back to your room," he said.

I continued to denounce militarism at my desk for the next few days, but under difficulties, for the tension grew worse. I had just written my final, stinging paragraph when my mother swept into my room. (Her entrances were always superb and were modeled on Mrs. Patrick Campbell.)

"Still scribbling?" she said and, bursting into tears, flung herself upon me, showering me with kisses and hugging me passionately.

Without apparently suspending her kisses and hugging for a moment (an art, again, I think learned from Mrs. Campbell) she managed to say, "Your father is jealous of *you,* his own son! Why shouldn't you love me? Why *shouldn't* you?"

I took a handkerchief from my breast pocket and offered it to her, and then, disentangling myself as gently as

I could, I said I would go and get her a glass of brandy. She took the handkerchief and nodded, but I thought I saw a flash of Irish temper in her dewy eyes.

When I came back with the brandy, she had collapsed on the bed. Her abandon was so marked that I was at first alarmed, thinking she might really be ill. But then I noticed that the act of collapsing had raised her skirts to her knees (she had very shapely legs) without disturbing a hair of her coiffure.

I set aside the brandy and then pulled down her skirts, averting my eyes, an act which made me feel like one of Noah's sons covering his father's nakedness. But therein is the tragedy of incestuous mothers: they make their sons feel feminine, which is the last thing they want.

I sat on the bed. I held her hand and stroked her forehead. She opened her eyes. She rolled over on her side and I felt that she was coming at me again. I seized the brandy glass and held it between us, and with this delicate instrument I tried to defend immemorial taboos.

She sipped a little, and we talked.

"Your father," she said, "is a good man."

The statement came quite naturally, for she had used it a hundred times in the course of bringing me up. It further lowered the temperature, for it is not a phrase that Heloise would use to Abelard, or Hero to Leander. "Menen, Menen, wherefore art thou Menen?" would have been more apt, but my mother did not read Shakespeare.

I took the opportunity to say that we should not hurt his feelings. The ambiguous phrase raised her hopes. She put her hand on my thigh and said, "No, we mustn't, must we?" and slid her hand further up my thigh.

It was now or never.

"And I thought all along," I said, "that he was angry about your flirting with Raman," naming the dandy.

She stared at me. Her eyes blazed.

"Flirting!" she said. "How *dare* you? What a way to talk to your own mother."

She banged down the glass, got to her feet and left the room, crimson in the face.

3.

I had a smattering of psychoanalysis gathered from some popularizing book I had found in the Public Library. I rather proudly told myself that I was in an "Oedipal situation," a nice new phrase in those days, and one to roll around the tongue. But it did not really fit my mother. She had an incorrigibly happy disposition and tragedy rarely lasted more than an afternoon with her. She would have been useless to the Greek dramatists, and Freud would have dismissed her as flippant. At any rate, the next day she was as sunny as ever. She was not possessive. She even asked me why I was hanging about the house on such a nice day. She bore me no grudge about mentioning Raman. She even played a gramophone record he had given her, dancing round the room by herself. It was called "I Kiss Your Pretty Hand, Madame." Raman was like that. He had a passion for *thés dansants,* which he considered the apex of Western civilization. I thought him a popinjay and a goose, but when as a fully grown man I lived years in India, I saw that he was right in his own way. Tea in India is drunk out of handleless brass cups with loud, appreciative sucking noises.

The situation, however, had a profound effect upon me. I persuaded my English master to lend me more books on psychoanalysis which I devoured because I could identify myself so excitingly with some of the central characters. I did, at times, feel rather callow. I could not, for instance, remember being envious of my father's penis. I could not recall ever having seen it. But my self-esteem was greatly restored when I discovered that, like as not, I would be a homosexual. This put me immediately in the company of Shakespeare, Michelangelo, Leonardo da Vinci, and, less encouragingly, Oscar Wilde. All boys of sixteen are homosexual, especially in schools where there are no girls. My special friend was a pretty blond boy, and I wrote him some poetry which began as sonnets but tended, in later lines, to blank verse in the style of Walt Whitman, another distinguished member of our company. I entitled them "To Mr. D. W." Mr. D. W. was very flattered, complimented me on my gifts and urged me to write dirty limericks. He copied my verses out, and, with a slight change here and there, sent them to his girl friend. I do not know what she thought of them because I broke off our budding affair.

4.

There was another difficulty. One does not think of a woman with an incestuous passion for her son as being fickle. It should be an all-absorbing and destroying love.

But it did not destroy my mother one bit. It came and went, and left her each time much as she had been before. It really depended on whether I did anything to arouse her. Thus weeks passed after her first attempt with nothing untoward. Then I won the 200-yards hurdling event in my school sports. The sight of her son flying through the air in abbreviated trousers revived her love, and for days afterwards she haunted my room, hugging and kissing me passionately, with other attempts which I grew expert at fending off. Going up to University left her cold for months (freshmen are invariably louts) until she saw me in the University Dramatic Society's annual play. In this I had the role of the boon companion of the young and dissolute Francis of Assisi. I bowled her over again, this time it being, I am sure, the particolored Florentine tights that I wore.

So it went on, throughout my life. The success of my first novel started quite a bout. She hugged me closely and whispered, "Hurry up and win the Nobel Prize before I'm too old." She saw herself, I knew, shaking hands with the King of Sweden, while the courtiers murmured, "But how can she be his mother? She looks so young." My first house in Italy, by the Tyrrhenian Sea, with three terraces of gardens, caused her to be periodically in love for years —each summer, that is, that she came out to stay with me. What with the wine, the sun, and the relaxed morals of Amalfi in June, she carried things too far in public. The old men on the stone benches in the piazza gave her a nickname: *la puttana,* the whore. Fortunately, she did not understand Italian.

5.

Some months after my father was put to rest under his rose tree, my mother went into hospital for an operation to deal with what we thought was a small matter. It was not. The surgeon found that she had a cancer in the pancreas. It could not be removed; it could not be cured. She had less than a year to live.

She was deceived by her doctors into thinking that she might get well. She recovered from the operation; her spirits were high and she was not in any pain that the drugs they gave her could not relieve. But each time she looked in the mirror she could see a piece of her beauty fade.

Then one day she came in from the garden and said to me, "I'm dying, aren't I? I can see it in your eyes when you look at me."

I took the flowers she had in her hand and laid them on a table.

"The doctors say nobody can be sure, Mother."

"Yes, they can. *You're sure.* I know it."

We faced each other, and I had no answer.

"Tell me," she said. "Tell me the truth. How long have I got to live?"

"Till February."

It was not so very difficult to say. She was, as I had always known, a woman of enviable moral courage.

Her eyes widened a trifle, as though peering into darkness. She showed no other sign.

"Thank you, my son," she said.

Then we embraced. I kissed her full upon the lips. We embraced as mother and son, and as nothing else but mother and son. It was the first time we had so embraced since I had ceased to be a child; and it was the last time.

She picked up the flowers and began to put them in a vase, her hands trembling a little. It saved her from crying, for I saw that her eyes were full of tears.

"Don't forget," she said, "that you've promised to take me to town and give me a lovely dinner and go to see *My Fair Lady*. I *do* want to see it."

She stood quite still, a flower in her raised hand. She was looking through the window at her garden, which she had always loved.

We never went to *My Fair Lady*. Her illness took a turn for the worse and she was carried off to a nursing home. She rallied, and they let her come back to the house and above all, her garden. Her face had withered. She would look into a mirror, and tears would run down the deep wrinkles. Otherwise, she did not complain. She would walk painfully down the garden path, stopping to examine her favorites among the flowers.

One day I heard her calling excitedly, "Kali, Kali, come and look at this. The peach tree is going to blossom again this year."

She was standing by a tree which she had grown from a peach stone she had saved from her first visit to Italy.

"Kali, Kali," she said again, "where are you? Come into the garden!"

She had forgotten he was dead, and I did not know what to do. Very slowly I walked down the path and stood beside her.

She turned, looked full at me, her eyes shining as brightly as they had ever done. She chattered on about the tree, seeing not me, but my father.

I took her arm, and began to walk her back to the house, for she was too infirm for so much excitement. When we got to the door, she put her arm, now painfully thin, around my waist.

"Yes," she said unexpectedly. "It's you. I knew it was you. Kiss me."

6.

That evening we had, once again, champagne, but she could only take a sip. The morphine pills they had given her in great quantities had temporarily stayed the pain. She looked at the picture of herself and began to talk of her youth—her lovers, the beauty contest, meeting

my father, their lovers' quarrels. Her lined face grew viv-
idly alive. She rambled on till she came to my birth, my
babyhood and my adolescence. She gave me a wanton
look, and then, slowly, she pulled her skirt above her
knees. She laughed, a light, young laugh, and a long one.

"I've had a happy life," she said.

She seized her stomach. Her laughter had brought
back the pain, and in a way, I suppose, it killed her. But,
after all, it was February.

She lingered in her hospital bed for a few days, long-
ing to die, and telling me so. She once asked me to take
her mirror from her handbag and let her see her face. Re-
luctantly, I did so.

She took one swift look.

"A hag, that's what I am. A repulsive ugly old hag.
Take the mirror home with you. I never want to see my
face again."

Next morning the hospital rang me. They asked me
to come with all possible speed.

She looked wonderfully composed, and some of the
fiercely scored lines had gone from her face. "I'm dying,"
she said in a tiny trembling voice. "Help me up. We must
say goodbye."

I took her thin and wasted body in my arms.

As I held her she said, her voice suddenly loud and
steady, "Why when you embrace me are you always so
cold?"

Then she made a little, complaining noise as the pain
returned and she grew pale. I laid her back on her pillow
and pressed the bell for the nurse.

She died that night, peacefully, they said, but then they always say that.

7.

Mr. Killick, with his long pointed shoes and his gift for a phrase, had the last word.

There had been no hitch in the funeral this time. We stood for a moment by the black limousine where it had pulled up outside the now empty house, with its deserted garden.

"Well," he said, "mother and father dead, sir. It's a watershed for you. It always is." Then, as he shook my hand, "And don't mistake me, sir, but I sincerely hope I don't see *you* for a long, long time."

8.

After the doll, the embrace, says my notebook. The doll no longer worried me. The doll had not made the boy who climbed the hill to see the burial mound, nor the man who sat in the colonnade of Mars Ultor, nor, above all, the man who sat alone in his room, dissecting his life. It had made the man who had written the banned play; it had made the writer of the row of my books which stood on the shelves of my room; it had made the man who had asked Gottlieb what it was all about, that day alone in the house. But the tranquil observer of all this that I had

found deep inside myself was no part of any of this. Secure
in this discovery, I could see the country girl dressing her
brown-faced doll as a figure to admire, a girl who knew
her own mind amidst her giggling bumpkin companions.
I could see, too, the woman who married her doll in the
shape of my father as the same woman who had faced the
news of her death with courage. The Upanishads had
taught me a lesson. When we judge others, we put ourselves in the heart of every judgement. It is how those others affect us, or might affect us, that makes us harsh or
gentle in our estimate of them. We do not let them be
themselves. Indeed, we do not know what those selves are
like. But once we have seen that our own lives are not our
own, and once we have discovered what is our own, and
once we know that those others can have no part in what
is our own, then all need of judging passes from us.

9.

But the memory of that cold embrace lay heavy upon
me, much as the scent of the funeral wreaths hung about
the house. The perfume disappeared, but not the memory. It was with me when I packed the boxes to send to
Gottlieb. It was with me when I handed the keys of the
house to the new owner who had bought it from me. It
was with me on the plane that took me back to Rome.

Why had I been so cold? Why had I been so *crass?*
Surely in her last hours on earth I could have given her a
moment of content.

There was another question, even more searching. As I had known for many years, when a person dies that has been much in your life, you always wish him back for a moment to put something right between you: a letter you did not write or a letter you should not have written, something foolish said in anger and soon repented. It is a lesson we all have to learn. We wish to be forgiven by the one person who cannot do it. We try the handle of the door to see if it will open just one last time, but it does not.

Yet I had no such feeling about my mother. If the door had opened and I could have embraced her once more I would have done it in the same cold way. I accused myself of hardness of heart and I believe that had I not shut myself away I would have felt this accusation weigh on me for the rest of my life. But I knew, deep within me, that it was something other than this, and this other thing I would not face.

I shut myself in more firmly. There comes a time in this experiment that I was conducting when the most fleeting contact with the outside world can bring it to ruin, especially if the contact is with human beings. I asked the janitor to buy the little food I was eating and put it on a marble shelf that was in the corridor. I shunned the bar and made my own coffee and it was so abominable that I made as little of it as I could. I was at last quite alone. Within six hours I found I had a companion.

10.

This experience was so crucial and so striking that I would wish to describe it well, but I do not know that I shall succeed. I must postulate a soul, or a spirit, though I cannot say just what it is. The Upanishads call it the *atman,* but to give it a Sanskrit name throws little light on it. It is not just the mind, for in my case my reasoning mind regarded it all with a mixture of skeptical caution and wonder.

This soul (a soul so self-assured it would be preposterous to think it needed saving), this *atman* withdrew, hour by hour, into itself, like an amoeba pulling in its pseudopodia. I felt I was falling into a deep sleep after a weary day. When that happens to us, we leave, one by one, the memories of our waking hours, our thoughts of tomorrow and our emotions. Next, little by little, we leave the room around us and the sounds of the world outside. Then we are asleep, unknowing.

Just so I seemed to fall asleep, but in the middle of a paradox: the more I fell asleep the wider awake I was. My mind had the lucidity of waking in the early morning and finding a problem solved. I was awake, but as tranquil as a child opening its eyes to a new day.

What I saw was myself, quite detached from me; the person who had been bored by a Pope, who had sat on the boxes containing his life, who had failed in his last embrace with his mother.

I had no feeling for him: no sympathy, no dislike, no need to criticize or praise. I had curiosity about him; not the hot curiosity with which we regard our fellow men, or with which we read something written by others about ourselves. It was the curiosity of a scientist with some new specimen: of Darwin on the Galapagos Islands, distinguishing the species of life he found, or of a geologist manipulating a rock from the moon.

Yet even that simile is misleading. A scientist investigates because he does not know what he will find. I knew all about that other person who was my outside self, outside in the world. I knew intuitively and I knew all. I was like those monads of Leibnitz, withdrawn into themselves completely, but reflecting everything in a pre-established harmony.

There was still one other thing. I knew but my knowledge was not explicit. Thus a pure mathematician may feel intuitively that he has hit upon the solution of some problem but to bring out that answer into the light of day he must construct equations and follow trains of reasoning until he can at last write down what had to be demonstrated, and which, all along, he knew he could do.

Should anyone else try the experiment I was making, I think it will be found that each person makes his knowledge explicit in his own way. With me, it was through a dialogue between my two selves, the one serene, the other twisting, evasive, but compelled to answer.

11.

"That cold embrace was the most honest act of your life, but you won't admit it."

"It was cruel, and I am not a cruel man."

"It was not cruel. You were quite glad she was dying. It was your final release from a tie that had bound you all your life."

"That's true, I suppose. But I should have hidden my feelings."

"I'm surprised you didn't. You've been hiding your feelings all your life."

"She brought me up to have good manners. She taught me that I must always have consideration for others."

"She brought you up to be a hypocrite. All parents do."

"What is so hypocritical about having consideration for others? How else can we all get on together?"

"Love your neighbor?"

"Yes. Why not? Why be so sarcastic?"

"Because you don't love your neighbor. You never did. You became a Christian because you thought it would help you do it. Did it?"

"No."

"You felt just the same about them, except that you felt guilty about feeling it. Right?"

"Yes. But at least it was a step in the right direction."

[77]

"If running away from yourself is the right direction. Because that is what you were doing. And you've been doing it all your life."

"How?"

"You've pretended to like people more than you do. You pretended to love them when you did not love them at all. Did you ever tell your mother to go to hell and leave you alone?"

"No."

"But that was what you wanted."

"Of course."

"That is what you have wanted from everybody but you will never admit it. You wanted your privacy."

"Well, yes. Yes, very much. It's a passion. It's almost a perversion. I mean, it's wrong. No man is an island."

"Every man, woman and child is an island. But other people insist on dragging them off it."

"Yes. Lovers especially. And husbands and wives, I suppose. That's one of the reasons why I never married. Still, there were lovers. I liked falling in love."

"But you liked falling out of love better."

"Yes. I got something of myself back—out of pawn, you might say."

"You remember that beautiful boy from Naples who looked like Antinoüs. At least you insisted he did."

"Franco. Yes."

"You remember the day he tapped your breastbone and said, 'I know what's going on here'? Then he tapped your forehead and said, 'But I wonder what goes on there.'"

"Neapolitans are all heart."

"They are brought up to be. So are we all, in some measure. People take a lot of trouble to teach us to love our fellow men when we are young. That's because our purely natural reaction to them would be to keep them at arm's length."

"Or give them a punch on the nose. Sometimes."

"Do you feel as badly as that about them?"

"I said 'sometimes.' Why do they want to devour me?"

"Because they devour one another."

"Right."

"But they haven't succeeded in devouring you."

"I'm not sure."

"But I am. And I am you. I sat alone in this room and found what you have been running away from all your life."

"Myself?"

"Your own private self. Your own island where no cannibal will ever draw up his canoe and come and get you for his cooking pot. So now you know why you gave your mother such a brief embrace. You were in a hurry. You were already on your way here."

"The watershed."

"Just so."

Chapter 6

YOUNG LOVE IN A DIPTYCH

1.

I am aware that I have botanized on my mother's grave. I think the seed of the habit was born with me, unattractive as that habit is. The seed was brought to flower in the silence and loneliness of Piazza Farnese, but it was there long before, and I think it was one of the things which led me to shut myself up in my room. I botanized on young love when I was a young lover, having sex with a woman for the first time.

2.

It was all as romantic as it could possibly be, and I owed it to my mother's love: her love, that is, not for me, but for Raman. My father had gone to Bokhara to buy antique rugs, for which he had an eye and London a market. My mother announced that in the meantime she and I would take a holiday in Paris. I knew it would be all right because instead of squeezing my arm and saying, "Then you and I can go shopping together," and giving me a kiss, she said, "Then you can go and see your stuffy old Louvre as much as you want." This recalled the time when I was first taken to Paris at the age of twelve and complained to my footsore parents we had only spent a single day in the museum. I was not at all surprised, then, to find Raman turn up, full of mock surprise, at the first *thé dansant* at our hotel. I should not have been in the hotel at all at that hour, but by chance it was a day on which the Louvre closed early. I met the situation with all the knowingness of seventeen years. I peeped into the pink-shaded tea lounge, saw Raman, turned on my heel and went off to see if I could still get into Napoleon's Tomb.

Paris is Paris and teatime is, after all, an English habit. I rather fancied that one day soon I would be packed off for my mother and Raman to have a night of love, but I wondered how it would be managed. Then one morning I saw my mother studying a poster in the foyer which announced the performances at the Opera.

"You should go to see the Opera," she said. "Everyone does in Paris. I won't come with you because I'm not feeling very well. But you go alone. I'll buy you a ticket." For one terrible moment I thought I would have to sit through *Hansel and Gretel*. But I suppose that the air of Paris was making me into a little man of the world. I gathered my wits together.

"Wonderful," I said. "Look, Wagner's 'Ring' begins

tomorrow. You remember. I listened to it on the radio last year. *Tomorrow* will be splendid."

"Oh," said my mother without any enthusiasm. "Oh, well. Here's the money. You get the ticket from the hall porter, and don't worry if he overcharges you. They always do."

Then she smiled a very happy smile and began to hum a current tango, from which I gathered that she had decided that keeping Raman waiting a night might be a good idea.

3.

It was a cold night, with a flurry of snow. Coming in from my taxi into the warmth, the Opera House seemed doubly luxurious. I looked open-eyed at the audience filing up the grand staircase, a piece of theatricality so triumphant that the actual opera never seems to beat it. I looked for my own more humble entrance (as I imagined) but I was waved up the staircase, a box was unlocked by a woman in a starched uniform, and I was shown inside. It was empty except, for a while, for the woman, who planted her feet apart and stood there till she was tipped.

The explanation was that it was a Wagner night and on such occasions the thrifty French subscribers to boxes had a habit of letting out the seats and discreetly staying at home. There was only one other ticket-holder.

She came in soon after. Her toilette was in the highest style. She glittered and sparkled so much that it was strange to see her alone, nor did I ever find out why she was. Perhaps she had quarreled over dinner with her escort. I waited for him to come, tense with boyish nerves at being alone in a box with a perfumed and jeweled woman. Soon it was apparent she was expecting nobody, because she smiled at me, said "Good evening," and dropped her program. I picked it up. She thanked me in French, I mumbled in English. "Not at all, not at all," at which she smiled and began talking to me, a little haltingly, in the same language.

I wonder if she really was as beautiful as I thought she was and as I still thought her right to the end of the affair. She was in her early twenties, with a smooth, regular face and expressive eyes. But I would be lying if I said I could really remember her. Yet I can still remember, very clearly, my astonishment at looking at her. Not so very long ago I had a tête-à-tête luncheon with Sophia Loren, during which she pointed out to me the defects in her face, a sure way of proving that she really had none. Sitting next to her afterwards in the car, and looking at her, I felt exactly as I had done as a boy, sitting in the box at the Paris Opera.

4.

The curtain, as ever, was late in rising. We had time to talk. She asked me what I was doing in Paris and I said, "I am reading Flaubert's *Salammbô*." Rather, I blurted this out in a mixture of embarrassment and a desire to make an instant impression.

"What do you think of it?" she asked.

"I think it very overdone," I said, then, instantly blushing, I cursed myself for a fool.

"Very good. *Very* good," she said. "Do you know that the Goncourt brothers wrote the same thing in their *Journal?*"

What prig of a seventeen-year-old boy could resist such a compliment?

"No, really?" I said. "What did they say?"

"They said it was ancient Carthage got out of Algerian bazaars."

We laughed. I was in love. I wanted to marry her so that we could have conversations like this forever and ever.

5.

The performance was very bad. Some of the singers, the chorus, the orchestra and the conductor were all French. The French singing Wagner are as unlikely as the Italians playing cricket. There was a conflict of temperaments between the composer and the performers. Towards the end the pace got quicker and quicker as though it were generally agreed that the thing should be got over with.

The curtain fell and Juliette and I clapped with equal languor. In the intervals we had found so much in common. Besides, I had managed to shoulder my way through the crowd at the bar and buy her a drink without waiting at all. And she had noticed it. And she had said so.

6.

The snow was falling more thickly when we got outside the theatre. I was about to say goodbye to her when she wailed, "I shall never get a taxi in this weather. Women never do."

I waved my hand. More magic: the taxi drivers proved as ready to serve me as the bartenders. One pulled up immediately in front of us. The doorman opened the door, saluted, and held the door wide open to the cold until I remembered I had to tip him. I unbuttoned my overcoat, found some money, gave it to him and we drove off.

"I shall see you safe home," I said.

"How sweet of you," she replied, looking not at me but at the front of my trousers, exposed by my open overcoat. Without raising her eyes, she told me her address. I leaned over to the window, told the driver, who started off at a great pace. I fell back into the seat and into her arms. We were not a hundred yards down the Avenue de l'Opéra before she was kissing me and I her.

I cannot recall where exactly we were when she began to unbutton my trousers. I remember trees, so perhaps it was the Bois de Boulogne.

7.

There was a large bookcase in her apartment, a curly affair with applied brass garlands. She left me alone there for a moment, and it was a bad moment for a young man on the verge of his first affair. I wondered rather desperately how one could discuss the Goncourt brothers with a healthy erection. I saw a book of drawings on a table and I decided I could put that on my lap.

Such tactics were quite unnecessary. She did not discuss the Goncourts: she did not even come back into the room. She was a very clever girl. She did not so much as offer me a brandy, which might well have recalled my mother with disastrous results. She simply opened her bedroom door and stood there quite naked.

A worldly-wise woman has since told me that this is the correct way to seduce adolescents: boys have a graceful way with their lips but are very clumsy with their hands. Even the most loosely tied ribbon can present them with a problem. Juliette presented no problems at all. She did not even shock me, but that was perhaps because of my priggishness. I told her she was lovely and that she looked just like the picture in the Louvre by Greuze called *La Source*.

"You mean," she asked, "that girl pouring water from a jug on her shoulder? Brr. It always makes me shudder. Think of all that cold spring water on a snowy night like this. Come: let's go to bed and get warm."

I went in and she immediately got into bed. It was now my turn to undress. I had, of course, thought about this moment, and I tried to do the thing aesthetically. I took off my jacket and shirt and vest first, and only then proceeded to take off my trousers. I had, however, forgotten to take off my shoes. There was a long moment of tugging and fumbling in a far from elegant position and a time of panic because I thought I was losing my erection. I do not think, as a matter of fact, that there is any really neat solution to the problem of taking off Western shoes. In the Orient they merely kick off their sandals, which may be the reason why they make love in so much more relaxed a way.

But soon I was naked beside Juliette. Her expertness aroused me: my lack of it did the same to her. We had sex together twice, the first time with passion on my part, the second time with less passion than pride. There was some disappointment. Coming was not the fountain of joy that I had expected, while Juliette's cries of ecstasy struck me as being a little theatrical. Nor did I find her admirably shaped body a source of mystery, as I had read men do. On the contrary, I found it remarkably functional.

But in that fact lay the joy that I felt. Sex had been so simple. Lying beside her, I felt that it was the one really simple thing which had happened to me in my complicated life. Everything had led me to believe that it would be a combat, a hot thing of desire and rejection, of fighting and surrender and, at the last, abandon. But it had been a simple coming together. I stared at her as she lay with her head on my shoulder. I stared at the ceiling with its white mouldings of swags of fruit and flowers. I think the best description of my feelings then was that I was converted to sex. I would do this simple, friendly thing all my life even—perhaps—why not?—with her. I fell lightly and happily to sleep and when I woke I found it was past four o'clock.

I dressed and made my way home. The snow had stopped. My magical touch had gone, too, because I waved at three taxis which all bowled past me. My feet began to get cold.

"*Tristesse,*" I said to myself, "always follows *l'amour,*" and immediately felt as French as La Rochefoucauld.

8.

Perhaps it was because my feet were so cold, but the full force of young love did not hit me until I woke up next morning. Then, however, it not only hit me; it battered me out of my senses. I was not concerned with having conquered a woman, as boys are supposed to be. I was delirious with the sensation of loving. I was overjoyed at finding I was not the cold fish I had begun to fear I was. My Juliette had saved me from being the sort of Romeo who would have argued that given the state of affairs between the Montagues and Capulets, prudence rather than raptures was called for. Under it all, I *was* that sort of boy. But not for the moment.

I rang Juliette as soon as I had fortified myself with coffee and *croissants*. I was in deadly fear that she would not answer, or would greet me with a rebuff. She answered me for about half an hour. We made an assignation. We were to meet at the café opposite the Palais Royal.

I arrived half an hour early; she arrived half an hour late. During the interval I passed from anxiety to panic. Had I mistaken the time? Had I got the place wrong? My waiter was a bald man who seemed very friendly. I asked him if there was another café to suit the description. There was not. Ten minutes later I asked him if a lady had enquired for me. No one had. Ten minutes later I called him over again and asked him if he had seen a lady looking like such-and-such. This time he answered very shortly, and retired glowering. A little later he came back and said that come to think of it, a lady like the one I had mentioned had been there at 3 P.M. and waited, and gone away very angry. Tears started to my eyes. I had mistaken the time. I felt I was choking, and then I saw Juliette.

I must have given her just the overjoyed reception she had hoped for. She apologized for upsetting me.

"It was that waiter," I said and pointed to him. He was grinning. "He told me you had come and . . . and *gone.*"

"*That* old bitch," she said, this time in French. Then, in her English, "He is homosexual. He doesn't approve of boys—young men, I mean, so sorry—going with women."

This was wonderful. It was Marcel Proust. I had been reading him, having gone backwards (as everybody did) from *Sodom and Gomorrah* to *Swann's Way*. I asked her if Albertine was a girl or really a boy. She gave her opinion but I could see that the conversation was taking a wrong turn for her.

"You read many, many books," she said. "Perhaps too many." She reached her hand across the table. "How would you look without your glasses?" she asked, and took them off. My mother used to do that, until I complained.

It was a shadow, no more than that of a swallow's wing on a sunlit wall. But it was a shadow.

9.

We met regularly. We had sex in the afternoon, not because it was how they did it in books, but because that was the time when *thés dansants* were held, and my mother never asked me what I was doing.

Besides, Juliette's evenings were often occupied. She was supposed to be studying for some diploma, but plainly she was some other man's mistress.

This did not disturb me. I asked no questions about him. The trouble was that she incessantly asked questions about me. She asked so many that I felt sure she would one day go on asking them while I was on top of her. She did not get as far as this, but she never waited for very long after I had got off.

She was immensely, envelopingly sympathetic. She was extremely excited about my writing and asked why I seemed cool towards it. I foolishly told her that my last three pieces had been rejected. I was overwhelmed with advice about sticking it out and refusing to be defeated. I was assured a dozen times that I would make my name. She clung to me and said, "You must, for my sake." This struck me as the silliest of reasons for making one's own name. I remember that I reached out to the bedside table at this point and put on my glasses with deliberation, Juliette still clinging to me.

Encounter followed encounter, and in each she grew more intimate, more solicitous for me, more deep in her probing. I had giving up going to the Louvre, but now I went there again, taking refuge in the Persian and Phoenician rooms, where nothing was interested in me at all, and I was interested in everything.

I had dodged all her questions about my parents. But one afternoon she told me how fascinated she was by the color of my skin. Since she had seen more of my skin than anybody I knew, I told her how I had come by it.

It was a disaster. From that day on she insisted that I had mystic depths in my eyes. Mystic depths got mixed up, later, with hidden sources of sexual powers. She was sure I worshipped Siva.

Finally I could stand it no longer. We were in bed, but I snatched her arms away, jumped out and, naked as I was, I told her that I wanted to be free of her. With that I went over to a chair and started dressing.

She was furious. She watched me, with her knees up under the bedclothes, and her chin resting on them.

"What are you doing?" she asked.

I replied, "I am putting on my trousers, and if you

can find anything mystical in that, I take off my hat to you."

She clenched her fists.

"What," she asked, "do you mean you take off your hat?"

"It is an English expression."

"A stupid, silly English expression," she said, beating her fists on the counterpane. "How can you take off your hat when you are putting on your trousers? Go *away*, you silly boy. Go *away*."

10.

We tried to patch it up in the café near the Palais Royal, but we had clearly quarreled, much to the waiter's satisfaction. Besides, my father was on his way back from Bokhara, and it was time to go home.

As the train left Paris I found myself crying, so openly that I had to go out into the corridor. I felt lonely, and no boy wishes for that. But the tears passed. By the time we reached Calais I was no longer lonely. I was alone, and that is a different matter, though it has taken me a lifetime to learn it.

11.

For the rest of my adolescence I was a problem for my intimate friends: a brief problem, it is true, for when they became intimate, I dropped them. At nineteen or so

I formulated a home-made psychology to explain myself to others. There was (I said) an area of privacy within everyone which, if it were invaded, made that person ill like a microbe, and he or she was not well until the microbe was ejected.

It was not well received. Where *was* this area, I was asked over milk and coffee in the Lower Refectory? In the Unconscious, the Subconscious or the Super-Ego? Was it not a Repression, a Complex, or an atavistic memory of the Tribe (this last from the Jungians)? I did not know. Nor did I know if it was a hideout to avoid my duties towards my fellow men (this from an unexpected alliance of Socialists, Communists and theology students). Was it not because I had a fear of women (this from a bright but ugly girl who increasingly felt fear of women accounted for a lot of mysteries around her)?

I began to feel a fool. I threw myself into the most gregarious activities, one of which (as I have mentioned) was the college theatrical society. I found this most congenial, especially since I was soon invited to work and produce my own plays. I formed a mildly physical friendship with a fellow student, partly because he had a charming face but much more because he was translating *The Bacchae* from the original Greek. He was a poet, dedicated to being immortal before he was twenty-five. He did not invade my private area at all. Indeed, I don't think he ever stopped to consider if anybody else but himself had one. As for his own, he was bursting to get T. S. Eliot to publish it to the wide world, and nothing would have pleased him better than to have it invaded.

It was at this point that I met Billy Green.

That was not his name, but the real one is just as resoundingly English. He was related to a family that had become famous in the days of Queen Anne, and was to have another illustrious scion in the war which, years later, left Billy Green dead in the Libyan desert.

Billy was forty, rich, and a *farceur*. English Billy should have an English epithet, but I have searched and there is none. A *farceur* is not a man who is fond of jokes. He is usually quite serious. But he loves to mystify: he loves strange habits and recondite cults. He aims to leave a disturbing impression among the bourgeoisie. He detests being understood.

Billy, too, was ahead of his times. He believed (or said he believed) in the worship of the gods of the Ancient Egyptians, with incense, prayers from the Book of the Dead, and the offering up of saucers of semen, this last item having no archeological foundation whatever. He also believed that there were primitive drugs that could enhance the perception. None whatever being available in England in those days, he made a long journey to Mexico with the sole purpose of collecting the fungus that produces mescalin—this, I may say, was at a time when Aldous Huxley was still grinding out unreadable best-selling novels and had not discovered the doors of perception.

He was quite unlike Juliette. He was fascinated by me, not because I had mystic depths, but because, as he said, I had nothing of the sort to the point of being cussed about it. My trouble, he insisted, was not that I was fear-

ful of having some private world invaded, but that I was a
prig who considered himself a cut above everybody else. It
was the result of having resisted my mother's advances. I
now set myself up as a judge of everybody else and found
them wanting. He said that I had no private world: I
was merely withdrawing the hem of my garment.

The solution was sex. He discoursed about the temple prostitutes in Canaan and other parts of ancient Asia
Minor. This would be a final release of all my inhibitions.
I should have sex in its most raw form. I would enjoy it,
and then know myself for what I really was. This was how
it had worked with the Canaanites.

I asked him how he knew that the Canaanites weren't
prigs, and he replied that of course they weren't and that
was what so infuriated the Hebrews. He then asked me to
spend a weekend at his house in Paris, at his expense.

12.

Everybody, including myself, has enjoyed the permis-
sive 1960s so much, it is perhaps a pity to point out that
they were invented more than thirty years ago. Billy
Green went on trips with drugs and he knew the Parisian
bars and night clubs where the young did their own
thing. The French, who are on the whole a dull and pro-
vincial lot, have no reason to look down on the Anglo-
Saxon. But the Parisian has. He invented the swinging
scene and now watches the world doing what he did, but
unfortunately with a great deal more chatter.

The place where I was to be pulled down from where I had set myself up was called "The Isis," a name naturally very dear to Billy. He warned me that a lot of the men I would see there were women and a lot of the boys would be prostitutes. What he did not say was that there would be two gendarmes in full uniform at the door. When I saw them I blanched and made urgent signs to Billy for us to go.

"It's been raided," I whispered.

"No, it hasn't," said Billy. "The police are there to prevent minors from entering."

"Ah," I said, "so the French draw the line somewhere."

"Not really," Billy said. "For little boys and girls they go to Morocco."

We entered and the gendarmes saluted the club's best customer.

In the foyer Billy said, "Now listen carefully. During the evening several very charming and good-looking boys will come and sit at our table. They are prostitutes. You will certainly refuse to believe that such healthy, fresh and innocent-looking lads can sell their bodies, and if you make that mistake it will only mean that they will take the shirt off you before morning. So, I want you to choose one and tell me which it is. No nods and winks and whispers. Say 'This one,' in French if you like."

He then took out his wallet and pulled out a large note.

"You will pay him this and not a centime more except for a *pourboire* which I shall tell you how to give. I shall pass you the money openly because it is a lot of money and I don't want your little friend to think you're a student or a tourist. Besides, it will help him choose the hotel.

"This hotel will be small, clean and supervised by a concierge. She will give you a broad smile. Do not jump to the conclusion she is laughing at you. She is simply a polite woman who likes to see business going well.

"The boy will take you to the room. Do not try to make conversation. He is not a geisha girl. In fact, I advise you to reserve all your talking till you get back to your young translator of *The Bacchae*. And for heaven's sake do not try to make love. He will do that."

"But suppose he doesn't like me. I mean, a boy has to be excited."

"He will be. Not with you, perhaps. But with the thought of this," he said, flipping the money. "It is, and always has been, the only reliable aphrodisiac there is.

"In the morning," he said, "you will take him to a café, but as you leave the room, you will give him the money. In the café, he will say that he works at a motorcar factory in Auteuil, that he is late, and he will have to take a taxi. He is not late because he does not work in a motorcar factory, but all the same you will give him the exact fare. Before he goes he will say that you are not like the other boys he has made love to: you are this, that and the other. He is trying to get a drink out of you. Do not yield. Now let's go into the club."

The room was large, with a dance floor and a small

orchestra. There were bright lights and virtually no decoration, as there is in most places devoted to the perversions. It seems that it is the normal man and normal woman who need lights, intimacy and luxury to arouse their passions. The wicked need only themselves.

The Lesbians were few in number, and the fact that they were there at all lends a period note to my description. Today, segregation has grown more strict. The Lesbians were richly dressed in evening attire, the girls in clinging, soft, feminine dresses, the men in fashion-plate evening dress. They gave off an air of intense respectability, as though they had left behind them at home a bonny family of offspring all sleeping in their little beds.

The boys were more raffish, one or two sporting workmen's clothing, such as overalls, a fashion invented, once again, I am sorry to have to record, thirty years ago by the Parisians. There were one or two well-heeled men of middle age like Billy.

The entertainment consisted of songs and dances. There was no nudity, that having held the public stage for years at the Folies Bergère. Instead, however, one or two of the performers were remarkable mimes, one in particular carrying on a telephone conversation with a friend while he explicitly masturbated an invisible client. He would nowadays be much sought after on Broadway.

As Billy had predicted, boys came and went at our table. They all found Billy intensely attractive, till he made a little sign with his finger, at which they all found *me* intensely attractive. If I am cynical now, I was not cynical then. I enjoyed the attention and believed it was genuine. I was in a very believing mood, for when one boy with flopping yellow hair and a turned-up nose arrived, I believed he looked exactly like Lord Alfred Douglas, the beloved of Oscar Wilde.

I told Billy this, with excitement.

"They all look like somebody," said Billy. "A whore is archetypal. His name is Claude."

I drank a glass or two and, by dint of imagining a straw boater on Claude's head, I saw him as Lord Alfred Douglas more and more. He had the same innocent eyes that I had seen in all the photographs. At about midnight it was Claude's innocent eyes that saw the money being handed to me.

All went as Billy had said. The concierge's smile was very happy, the sheets very clean. Lord Alfred Douglas made love to me. It was simple but good. As the *Encyclopaedia Britannica* knowingly remarks, anal intercourse is far less frequent in homosexuality than is often imagined.

In fact, this was one of Lord Alfred Douglas' main staples of lunchtime conversation. The real Alfred Douglas, that is, for a year or so later I met him, because I had been commissioned to write a play about Oscar Wilde. He was sixty, with an exceptionally ugly bulbous nose. He talked smoothly and at length: his price, as all London knew, was four hundred pounds to have his name mentioned without a lawsuit. As he talked, I thought of Claude.

"Oscar and I," he had said, "never committed sodomy. Never."

Nor did we. That is not the way a boy's body is taken; that is the way it is used; and his body was so beautiful, that my own—my muscles, my blood, all the mysterious chemicals that flowed in me, they were not needed. My penis rose like a charger and carried me into battle, brooking no rein. I had no thoughts. For the first time in my life my mind scurried away and sat crouching in some dark corner. All that concerned me at that moment—if indeed I existed—was that my nipples should press on his, our mouths should meet, groin crush upon groin and legs entwine.

That this encounter of bodies should result, again and again, in sex seemed an infantile interruption—for the sensations of sex are infantile, though we do not like to admit it.

I did not love him: I had no need to love him. Our bodies took each other and the morning stars sang together. It is that secret which, when we grow old, we begrudge the young.

Claude and I slept in each other's arms until morning. Claude smiled a lot, mentioned the weather once or twice, took his money, and we made for the bar. He asked me no questions; he did not think I was mystic. In fact, I do not remember him saying one really long sentence except that he worked in a motorcar factory in Auteuil and since he was late he would have to take a taxi.

13.

"And that time, what did you think of it all?"

"I thought it was the solution to all my problems. I had sex without being devoured."

"*Yes. He didn't make use of you. You made use of him.*"

"I saw that later."

"*And what do you see now?*"

"It is no solution to the problem."

"*There is no solution in other people at all. You find it in yourself, or nowhere.*"

Chapter 7

THE BEAUTIFUL PEOPLE

OF BLOOMSBURY

1.

So much for my growing up. Now it was my task, as I sat in my room, to examine myself as a young man, and that I found full of traps. We look back on our youth as the time, maybe the last time, when we were truly ourselves, bold, daring and original. After that the world takes over and rubs us into a smooth and fitting pattern.

The truth, I found (after many self-deceiving failures), is quite the opposite. When we are young we are the prisoners of our friends. We may rebel against the old, who will soon be gone and forgotten. We do not rebel against our boon companions, who will be with us and influence us all our lives. True, when we are young we have sudden moments of doubt. We push them aside and go forward.

If I were young and had those moments of doubt

again, I would go away alone and think about them. For the young, to mistrust one's friends is the beginning of wisdom. For I discovered in my room that it was in those doubting moments that I came near to my true self. I had a glimpse, as it were, of the Promised Land, which is the space within the heart.

2.

After Claude, I left my home after many scenes with a heartbroken mother and went to live on Charlotte Street with some money which my father gave me in the hope that it would keep me away from the house.

In the 1930s Charlotte Street was a sort of forerunner of Greenwich Village, and it looked very much as Greenwich Village looks today, until it was largely destroyed by air raids. Old houses had been turned into studios or cold-water walk-up apartments. The young people who inhabited these places defied convention in their dress (they wore corduroy, then the mark of the British workingman), they wore their hair long, and their gods were the Bloomsbury set—Maynard Keynes, Virginia Woolf, Lytton Strachey, and the others. The literary giants were invisible, but Maynard Keynes would sometimes ask the young of Charlotte Street to tea, Bloomsbury being just on the other side of Tottenham Court Road. One of the set, the painter Duncan Grant, actually lived among us, on our very road.

Occasionally to be found in this studio, a year or two

before I arrived, was a talkative man with a red beard. He
was D. H. Lawrence, and if the Bloomsbury group were
the gods of Charlotte Street, he was its prophet. But he
had soon disappeared to foreign parts in a chariot of fire,
pouring out the vials of his wrath on the ladies and gentlemen of Bloomsbury, accusing them of being snobs.

But then, like most prophets, he had a short temper.
One of the places he disappeared to was Taormina. After
he was dead I rented the small house outside the town
walls which he had occupied. A small marble plaque on
the walls would have beautifully enraged him because it
said "D. K. Lawrence lived here," the local tombstone
carver not being an accurate man. It had been paid for by
a local English resident who liked the man's books but
thought him impossibly vulgar. It has amused this bene-
factor to leave the plaque as it was for many years. Lawrence had left behind him an enduring memory. The
mayor of Taormina, hearing he was a distinguished English writer, had called upon him. He found him stark
naked, scrubbing the floor.

Nakedness was not the only fashion that he started.
He did phallic drawings which were exhibited in London
until the police closed the gallery: he wrote the first poem
in history to masturbation, his own masturbating, be it
noted. Martial had written about other people doing it,
but not about himself. Further, he had written the first of
what we nowadays call dirty novels, *Lady Chatterley's
Lover*.

We thus frequently went around naked in our rooms
and studios in Charlotte Street, the boys, curiously, being

more apt to do this than the girls. We read *Lady Chatter-ley* in editions smuggled in from France, and above all, we maintained that any form of sexual self-expression was legitimate. I myself talked much of writing a very witty play about Diogenes who, as well as living in a tub, masturbated in public to show his contempt for human beings. But the idea did not meet with much approval from my companions, who said sex was too important to be treated cynically. Diogenes, they said, should masturbate from the joy of sexual release, something I failed to imagine him doing.

I was not, in fact, a devoted Laurentian. Lady Chatterley reminded me a little too much of my mother. At least it seemed to me that she did at the time, and not for anything in the world will I read the book again to check if this was true. I was more of the psychoanalytic camp. Freud, Jung and Krafft-Ebbing were very much in the air. We did not believe that sex was beautiful. But we were sure it should be uninhibited by Mosaic laws of the permitted and the forbidden. Freedom was all. Our favorite story to shock the visiting bourgeoisie (anxious parents, prurient uncles) was that the famous philosopher Bertrand Russell was running a school in the country where if a little boy or little girl wanted to say "fuck" he would say it, in public and in front of the teachers.

Pioneers, o Pioneers, how you enjoyed yourselves, myself not the least! But I had to be careful. I felt that all my problems were over, dissolved as it were in semen. The day would come when nothing would cause anxiety or dismay or repulsion—not even perhaps incest. But this last I kept to myself. It was a subject, I found, which caused embarrassment.

3.

Although we talked incessantly about sex, we did not have a lot of it. An undergraduate who passed briefly among us remarked that more actual sex took place at Oxford with the skivvies, probably, he opined, because the boys up there lived higher on the hog. Way-out experiments in sex were rare, and not really understood.

A young woman who professed very advanced views about homosexuality once complained that she did not actually know what went on between two men. Full of my new-found freedom, I offered to let her watch. My current friend and I made love on a camp bed by a gas fire while she watched, glancing up occasionally from the pages of a book in a very ladylike way. A week later she stole my boyfriend, and they had a most satisfactory affair together. But it would be wrong to convey that such goings on were typical, or that I repeated them myself.

In fact, I settled down with my friend who was still translating *The Bacchae* from the Greek. It was a mild marriage. We settled the contract sitting on a bench in St. James' Park. He would live with me on one condition. If I got a book published before he did, he would never speak to me again.

The gods of Bloomsbury began to fail me, too. It was not that I found they had feet of clay: rather, their feet were exquisitely shod in expensive hand-made shoes and always rested on thick-pile carpets. They were as well-bred as racehorses; they even spoke in a whinny. It was known as the Bloomsbury accent and it was most ingenious. It enabled one to say modest and self-effacing things in a crushingly superior way. A lot of it remained with me for years until New Yorkers knocked it out of me.

Maynard Keynes was a soft but large man; he was charming with the young, a sure sign, of course (though we did not know it then), that the young charmed him. He was very eager to introduce us to the finer things of life—pictures, music, the ballet. Like the Sitwells, he was convinced that he had all the qualities of a civilized man, but with one drawback. He was English, and again, like the Sitwells, he thought the English were barbarians. Impeccable taste in all things artistic was therefore required of anybody in the group. It sometimes produced a sense of strain, like listening to a man being extra careful not to drop his "h's."

It was all to a very good purpose. One of his protégés was a small man with a hesitant voice who would take us, again at teatime, round his house and show us the Cézannes, the Van Goghs and the other post-impressionists that crammed his walls. This little man was Roger Fry, who singlehanded had taught the British that painting did not end with Rembrandt.

Yet I was not grateful. For one thing, I was not a barbarian waiting to be washed of my woad. The museums of Europe had been a place of refuge and cool repose for me since I was a little boy. Again, I was not English. However high I rose in the creative arts, I would not be what they were looking for. The whole trouble was that there were far too many talented foreigners and far too few British ones, and I knew this. Keynes' wife was foreign, a ballet dancer of some past renown called Lopokova. She would single me out as we sat round and give me a long, speculative stare. We were two strangers within the gates.

4.

Besides, I grew suspicious both of Bloomsbury and Charlotte Street. Goodness, kindness, understanding and above all tolerance were the order of the day, either in the drawing rooms or in the studios. Cruelty was abhorred, in any form. Violence was unmentionable. It was the loftiest view of human nature imaginable: so lofty, I began to think, that it looked clean over its head.

Then came sad proof that I was right. My young friend completed the first few chapters of a novel. It was natural to submit it to Virginia Woolf, a remote woman of whom one had only occasional glimpses. But one understood she was the acme of kindliness and understanding.

Back came a letter of rejection from her. It did not just say "no." It slashed and probed and cut until any hope the young writer may have had was a bloody mess on the floor. My friend was a poor boy of poor parents who had won his education in scholarships. He read it and he burst into tears, as every sentence and every word of the letter intended he should do.

The letter was taken to the painter, Duncan Grant. He shook his head sadly and said, a little mysteriously, that he would put it right. A week later another letter arrived, still saying "no," still signed by Virginia Woolf, but gentle, understanding, encouraging and, in a word, pure Bloomsbury.

My curiosity was aroused. The first had been the letter of an envious, uncertain, vain and uncontrolled woman. The second was in apple-pie order. Why? I was rebuffed on all sides. I was rude to ask.

It is all clear today. She wrote letters like her first, habitually, to young writers, unless some alert person stopped her in time.

I began to think that Charlotte Street and Bloomsbury could give me few lessons in human nature. I did not know what it was, but I knew it was not the beautiful thing I was being asked to believe.

5.

"But you had no courage. You conformed. You adopted the whinny and you went around talking sweetness and light and tolerance and being a hypocrite. Why? You were as near the truth as you had ever been."

"And more confused than I had ever been. How did I know that there wasn't something wrong with myself?

Some twist in my nature that made me see things in a distorted way?"

"*Coward.*"

"I was afraid, yes."

"*You were afraid of yourself, of your own mind, or
the very heart of you. To be afraid of other people is
often wisdom: to be afraid of yourself is merely cowardice.
Or perhaps it is just being young.*"

"Let us say it is that. But I *did* leave them all, at
last."

6.

What had begun to worry me was that all my friends
insisted that I behaved as though our wet pavements and
trampled leaves were the streets of the New Jerusalem. By
moving into the postal district of West Central 1, human
nature had become suddenly kind, instantly loving and
good overnight. I tried to believe this. But there was not
only Virginia Woolf to the contrary, there was my own
world of escape, the one that took me into the ruins of the
past. I had not enough money to go on expeditions, but I
had a ticket to the Reading Room of the British Museum
and the Museum's own vast galleries to wander among.
History, as I saw it, was largely a tale of horror mitigated
by art.

Nor was it always mitigated. The seats in the Reading Room were becoming harder to get as it filled with
refugees from Germany, striving to finish books, or to

start a new career, or just to keep warm. There was Norbert, a professor from Frankfurt with a remarkable facial resemblance to a Junker. He was working on a study called "On the Processes of Civilization." He was an amiable, scholarly man who had the humane idea that history could be written in a new way. The important question, as he would say, feeding the pigeons at lunchtime, was when men and women stopped sleeping in the raw and took to nightgowns. When he was in the middle of this fascinating research, it turned out that the important question was that he was a Jew. He escaped with his life and only half of his manuscript. His family did not escape at all.

He made my problems sound very small, and I told him so, as I fed my share of the mob of pigeons behind the Eastern Island statue of Hoa-haka-nana-ia. But he would not hear of it. It was important that my generation found out who we were before somebody came banging on the door at midnight and told us. Norbert advised me to give up reading archeological journals and to read anthropology. There, if anywhere, the secrets of human nature would be found.

I did as he advised and made copious notes, in a rather Germanic fashion, for Norbert had insisted that I narrow my field. I chose the occurrence of the color red in primitive ritual and image, a topic which turned out to be as vast as the terrestrial globe.

It was also very boring and from time to time I would take long walks alone round the squares of Bloomsbury under the plane trees. I began to think about myself and who I was, as Norbert had said, but this did not please Norbert at all.

"Zis," he said, in his heavy German accent, "is not thinking. It is egotism. You must see yourself in the social structure. Vot is your part in this social structure? Vot is your duty to the social structure? 'Ow can you improve this social structure?"

He threw the last crumbs of his sandwich at the pigeons and then shooed them away.

"Vot is that nursery rhyme you say here? Little Horner ... Little Jack ..."

"Little Jack Horner."

"So! You cannot sit in your corner and say 'Vot a good boy am I.' "

"I was beginning to think I was a rather bad boy."

"Egotism, still egotism. You are not just you. You are part of the social structure."

It was a new idea then. It was in the air in all the Bloomsburys in Europe. It has now become a commonplace in talking to the young. The words have changed. "Social structure" has become "the community," "the group" or, more grandly, "mankind." But whatever the words, they are still wrong. It is the purpose of this book to show how wrong they are.

7.

Still, I tried. I took my first steps towards inserting myself in the social structure by walking from Blooms-

bury down Kingsway to the Strand. There I stopped at
No. 76. I climbed some rickety, dark stairs to a shabby office on the top story.

There, sitting at a battered roll-top desk amid a confusion of papers, was an old friend. He was an Indian
from my father's birthplace. He was tall, with a great
shock of hair. Two piercingly black eyes were separated
by a bold, beaklike nose with the widely flaring nostrils of
the southern Indians. I thought, as I had thought many
times before, how handsome he was.

So did many of the advanced women of Bloomsbury.
I cannot say his face was his fortune. He had not a penny
to his name. But with the aid of his admirers he put together a little propaganda organization to fight for Indian
freedom from the British, and to fight in Britain. Years
before, when little better than a schoolboy, I had helped
him. We did not talk much about India. But he was con-
sumed with the ambition to be the first real Indian member of the British Parliament, and this attracted me. It
was such a preposterous desire: he was black, he was
broke, he had no influential friends and his Indian background was thoroughly obscure. Looking at his magnificent profile I would think of the young Disraeli: someone
asked what his ambition was, and the Jew Disraeli had instantly replied "To be Prime Minister." His questioner,
shocked, had said, "My dear boy, that won't do at all,"
but, of course, it did.

Disraeli, however, had married money. My friend, for
all his women admirers, was as chaste as a new-spurred
knight. It added greatly to his fascination, but not much

to his belly. V. K. Krishna Menon was often a very hungry man.

He was pleased to see me. We went to a cheap restaurant. I told him that I wanted to do something useful for society and I would like to help his India League again. He suggested we did some public speaking together as we had done before. Then suddenly he said, "Why did you side with Fenner Brockway that day?"

The intensity of his expression took me aback. Fenner Brockway was a maverick socialist member of Parliament whom nobody took seriously, in or out of the House. "That day" had been a committee meeting on a subject of such triviality that I had forgotten what it was; it was on the level of arranging a dance in some suburban hall to raise funds. But something had come to a vote and Krishna Menon had lost.

"I ... ah ... I," I said, "I don't think I supported anybody."

Menon's eyes blazed.

"You didn't vote, I know. But don't you see that *abstaining* was the equivalent to backing Brockway?"

"Did it matter?"

"You are very young," said Krishna Menon. "When are you going to mature?"

I knew what he meant. We had had this fight before. I had stumped England with him, from north to south, sometimes on the same platform, but more often alone at meetings which he could not make (for he was much in demand). We spoke for no fee save our train fare. Menon was fiery, voluble and unhappy. I was cool, measured and

thoroughly enjoyed it all. I liked the tricks of the trade—
the dull preamble ("Let them get a good look at you" as
one party organizer had told me); the solicitous attention
to the first interruption ("Never skewer him; the audience
will put you down as a bully") and above all I enjoyed
saving up my most telling points until after 10 P.M. when
the pubs closed and the hall filled. After a few pints of
beer the Englishman wears his heart on his sleeve, and
that was the moment for my big set piece on the Amritsar
massacre when General Dyer had shot down unarmed Indians. Above all I enjoyed the big rallies in Trafalgar
Square—the banners, the cheering, the rhetoric. I would
await my turn at the primitive microphone, leaning up
against a great bronze lion, relishing the spectacle and
wondering how Landseer could have managed to be such
a bad sculptor.

Menon felt that on these occasions he was not at his
best. But these rallies and meetings had to be organized
and that was done in committee meetings in London.
There Menon shone. He had enormous skill in pitting
one member of the committee against another. When he
had fanned the battle to the exact temperature he required, he would step in. After a few minutes the result
was clear: the winner was V.K. Krishna Menon. He spoke
far better on these occasions than he ever did on a platform. I admired his skill, and when the meeting was over,
I noticed that the result was always one step, however
small, on Menon's way to the top.

Now, sitting opposite him as he finished his cheese
on toast, older if not maturer, I saw that this was a man

after Norbert's heart. Here was someone who was inserted into the social structure with a vengeance, and inserted in the only way possible—to use it to climb it. And I saw it was not for me. I did not see clearly. I was still young. I was not myself. I was what the world and my friends had made of me. But hazily, as in an out-of-focus movie, I saw that if I followed Menon I would never be true to my own real being, even if, then, I did not know what that was.

So I did not follow him. I did not see him again until a decade and more later, when, as the High Commissioner for India, he had achieved the rank of Ambassador. He invited me to a grand ambassadorial lunch with some twenty of the great names of the land. He bore himself well; almost too well, I thought, for some of the fire had gone out of his eyes. When the lunch was done he signaled to me to be the last to say goodbye. We walked together through the ambassadorial halls and down the staircase towards the long black car of protocol that he had called for me. On the way doors were opened by flunkies. As we stood on the pavement, I said, "Well, well, Krishna. Liveried manservants."

His eyes instantly lit up.

"Yes. And they hate me. They hate my guts. But I'm on my guard; I'm on my guard."

I was very pleased. All the ambassadorial splendor had not dimmed his love for a fight. He would win, I knew: the flunkies would be sorry.

At the car door he said, "And how are you doing?

What is it like, writing books? I always wished I had been a writer," he said.

"And I always wished I had taken up politics, when I had the chance, years ago," I said.

We shook hands. Never had two old friends lied so valiantly to each other.

8.

The social structure, then, was not for me. Blooms-bury, too, was coming to an end. One day my father climbed the rickety stairs to my attic in Charlotte Street. He looked small and nervous. I offered him some gin in a teacup without a handle and he drank it eagerly.

Then he handed me a large manila envelope, marked only with a number. Inside were a dozen sheets of closely typed paper. It was a report from a private detective, and there they all were, my friends from Billy down to the girl who had watched me in bed, with names often misspelt and all wallowing in a mélange of plain lying and misunderstood facts. But there they were.

I read the paper through. I asked him if he wasn't ashamed of himself. He said, "Your mother is so worried. She can't sleep at nights thinking about you. She wanted to know what you were doing. I said you were sowing your wild oats but she flew into a temper. You know your mother's temper."

The world seemed to slam open the door of my attic

and pour into the little room, filling it with the stench of concupiscent bodies, dribbling the saliva of unwanted kisses over my books and papers.

"Have you shown anybody this?" I asked.

"Not yet."

"I could tear it up, you know. But I don't like drama," I said. "And what is it, after all? A maidservant with her eye glued to a keyhole."

"I don't like it myself," said my father.

"But you paid for it. A lot, I hope."

"Look," he said, "why don't you come home for a while? You could explain things."

But here was something that no walk through a museum or across the downs could protect me from. I would have to make a longer journey, a journey in reverse of that which my father had made.

"I'm planning," I said, "to go to India. But I have no money and I do not know what I shall do there."

My father jumped to his feet.

"A splendid idea," he said. "Come, let's get out of this room and have a meal somewhere."

During the meal he seemed to grow larger. He behaved exactly as a father should. Money would be found, and as for what I would do, was not the Nawab of this and the Maharajah of that a friend of the family? I could stay with them, write a book, a play, anything. He was a man of influence, in India.

"All's well," he said as he paid the bill, "that ends well."

9.

But it was not ended. I stayed with the Princes. I ostentatiously began a book. Then, one day, at the right moment, I disappeared into that vast country. I destroyed my father's and my mother's letters. I warned my friends not to tell them where I was.

There is a curious monument to that time lying on the desk in front of me as I write. It is my father's will, in his own neat and cramped handwriting. He had made it when I had disappeared.

He leaves his property to my mother, and at her death, "to my son, whose last known address was Grindlay's Bank, Bombay, India."

I can see now the anguish I must have caused him. But looking at the young man who did it as I sat in my room in Piazza Farnese, for the first time I approved of him.

"*That was well done,*" I said. "*You took your first step in finding yourself. Till then, you had been finding other people, and that is something you can spend a lifetime doing, to very little profit. You had taken your first step to here.*"

Chapter 8

I TRY TO BE GOOD

1.

I was on the path, but before I arrived in Piazza Farnese, I made two deviations, much stranger than the deviations I have described. I took up first good works, and then religion.

Once I had freed myself from my parents, my life became much more simple and successful. I did not write them again until the Germans began dropping bombs all around them: all I wanted to know was whether they had been hit. Meantime, I had resumed my writing of plays. There was no theatre in India, but the radio was much listened to. The British Raj was coming to an end. I merely took up the style of "Genesis 2" and adapted it for the air. I wrote a play for a dinosaur and a mammal. The dinosaur, a tired and pompous character, spoke with a British accent, the mammal with an Indian one. The mammal told the dinosaur about what the future held for both of them. The Indians, who had forgotten they had a sense of humor, were delighted. The Very Top Dinosaur in New Delhi listened in his stately palace while he dined, and I alleviated his boredom. I was given my own time on the air and told to do as I liked with it.

I had not entirely escaped (nor have I ever done so). I was, just as Solomon had said, interpreting one culture to another, the West and the East. When the West went to war, I interpreted every day until I collapsed with yellow jaundice. When finally, the Dinosaurs packed up their bags and waddled off, I was a well-known and well-paid mammal.

2.

Yellow jaundice is supposed to give one a very sour view of human beings. It had the opposite effect with me. I nearly died with it. When I returned to the living, I had a beard and an overwhelming desire to do good to my fellow men. I had reached the age of thirty. My previous life seemed to me to be cold, egoistical and depraved. I was not, I noted, suffused with love for humanity, but I thought it high time I was. I determined to be suffused, or bust.

I gave up all my writing, both for the radio and the films. I decided to go into the jungle and live among a primitive, backward tribe. There was a post going for someone to do them good by setting up village schools and such. I took it.

3.

The tribe that I went to live among were called the Dangis. They were a peaceable group of semi-naked savages who had lived in a teak jungle north of Bombay since the time before history. Hindus, Moslems and British had all invaded the country that surrounded their jungle, but the Dangis had been left alone. They had two weapons with which to defend themselves, the bow-and-arrow, and the anopheles mosquito. They used their bows to shoot lizards, from which they made a dish to which they were very partial. They left it to the mosquito to lay low any intruders, and the mosquito had obliged, for centuries. From time to time it also laid low a Dangi or two, but never enough of them to wipe them out.

They were a cheerful lot, much given to dancing and getting drunk on a liquor they made themselves from the jasmin flower and which tasted exactly like a weak martini. They somewhat languidly cultivated clearings in the jungle to provide themselves with just enough food to live on. They knew nothing of the outside world and did not want to know. They found the jungle as fascinating as a duke finds his lordly acres, but they treated it purely as an entertainment. They had none of that rather oppressive wisdom of the Red Indian: they were poor trackers—they did not eat meat and had nothing with which to kill the forest game—they had no jungle lore, and if they got lost (which they sometimes did) they would sit down and yell till somebody heard them, just like you and me. Voltaire believed that a simple savage was a happy, candid and goodhearted man. He was subsequently much laughed at. But, as in so many other things, Voltaire was right. The Dangis were the happiest people I have ever known. I did what I was paid to do. I set up a school among them but it was the Dangis who taught me a lesson.

One day a young Dangi dropped dead. It was clear to me that he had died of tertiary malaria, the plague of the forest, to guard against which I had filled myself with newly discovered prophylactics. The Dangis, however, were of a different opinion.

A day or two later, a sort of town meeting on the subject took place on the broad field in front of my bungalow. I sat on the verandah and listened, the one man in the place (my servant) who could speak both Hindi and Dangi translating the proceedings for me.

I had no alternative but to watch and listen because the Dangis had taken my acetylene lamp to light up the proceedings.

It was a sort of coroner's inquest. The verdict was soon reached, but that was only a beginning. The young man had died of Natural Causes. The real problem was to find out what he had done to get Natural Causes so annoyed with him that They killed him. Natural Causes lived in certain peculiarly shaped rocks, a number of well-known trees, a mountain spring, and in tigers. Provided Natural Causes were kept in order, they did nobody any harm. If they were allowed to go their own way, anything could happen.

The Dangis had a system for dominating Natural Causes, and they were as proud of it as we are of our ability to defy gravity and send men to the moon. Their scientists were certain women, of all ages, who had a profound knowledge of magic. They were not crones or eccentrics. They were perfectly responsible working women, ready, like doctors, to serve the Community at all times, which they did by going into trances, a rather painful business of rolling the head about, foaming a little at the mouth, and then coming up with the right set of magical equations to keep Natural Causes in order. They greatly resembled the dignified Mambos of Haiti, high priestesses of voodoo, who are always carefully addressed as "Madame," even by members of the Haitian government. But Indian primitives have a certain skeptical cast of mind. While no Mambo would ever be thought to be wrong, the Dangis allowed that there could be bad witches, in the terms of being incompetent, or ill-prepared, or lazy. These they hung up on trees upside down and beat with sticks. The good ones were rewarded with food, alcoholic drink, clothes and trinkets. These gifts were considered essential to the practice of any witch's profession.

Witches were not hastily judged. If a tiger, for instance, came out of the jungle and ate a man, it was not immediately assumed that the witch who specialized in keeping tigers happy was to blame. The man who had been eaten might have been at fault. He may not have provided her with sufficient presents. Thus, among us, the hastier critics will say that scientists, for all their airs, have not discovered a cure for the common cold. Wiser heads will point out that we have never provided them with sufficient funds for research.

This was the question that was being threshed out by the light of my acetylene lamp. The man had died in a fever. Fevers, it was well known, emanated from certain curiously shaped red rocks that were found here and there in the surrounding jungle. These rocks were usually quiescent, but if not controlled by the correct formula, they would, spitefully, give off a fever which would be caught by a passerby. To control them was, admittedly, a difficult task, far more difficult than controlling tigers. Tigers had been so brought under subjection that they ate only one man or baby every two or three years. Fevers were more frequent, but the witch who struggled with this problem had a reputation for hard work and sincerity. Had the young man who died done his duty by her?

An ancient of some fifty years (a great age in a jungle where the anopheles mosquito lived in every pool) was sure that he had not. He had been a flighty type, always in girl-trouble, and wasting his substance on them. He had nothing left with which to give the correct presents to the witches. The old man had sighed and said that when he too was young, he had felt that paying witches was a burden, but now, after a long life, he had learned the wisdom of it.

The elder brother of the deceased now spoke up, a plethoric man, for all his small size. He angrily denied the accusation. His brother had been carefree in his ways. But his family were respectable. They had never lacked in their duties or their gifts, and he himself had taken care of being extra generous to cover his brother's shortcomings. But that had nothing to do with it. It was about time that they all faced up to the fact that things were going to the dogs, and the witches could do nothing about it.

He glanced at me and said something that was discreetly not translated, but I gathered that my arrival was part of the general decline. He then listed a number of instances in which things had gone wrong *in spite of gifts to the witches*. He had kept tabs on the tribe's misfortunes and he now rolled them out with passion. The recital was followed by an uncomfortable silence.

A rather effeminate young man said in a high voice:

"Why go on and on? You know that to talk about one piece of bad luck means another will follow."

But he was brushed aside by the elder brother, who now squarely laid the young man's death on the shoulders of the witch, whom he described as lazy and grasping. His fervor roused others in the group to join his point of view. Supporters of the old man's argument began to protest. Voices were raised, fingers were flourished under noses. The meeting grew very noisy.

I wish I could report the conclusion of the debate, but I cannot. After a while, my interpreter grew so incensed by something that had been said, or, rather, shouted, that he left my side, and squatting down with the others in indignation, he joined in the fray.

Voices and tempers began to rise still further, until it came to what we would call blows, except that Dangis never strike one another. They push and shove the adversary in an insulting manner. After a great deal of this had gone on, the acetylene lamp was knocked over, and the meeting broke up in disorder.

4.

I went to bed thinking of the best way to teach the Dangis about the anopheles mosquito. I dreamed of my mother. There was an air raid going on (though the war had been over for some time) and she was, as usual, trying to make love to me.

I woke suddenly. It was quite dark. I groped for an electric torch and went to the verandah, flashing it here and there to frighten away the snakes. The jungle was vast and silent, the air quite still. I felt a curious clarity seep through me, like a crystalline liquid. My mind cleared, my vision cleared, my skin seemed washed of every impurity. I said aloud, "You bloody hypocrite."

Something scuttled away in the bushes, and the jungle was still again.

I have been told that a very bad dose of tropical jaundice, caught in the tropics themselves, takes many months to leave the body, but when it finally does you are healthy as never before. I do not know if this is true, but perhaps it was this that had happened to me.

I saw as never before that what I was doing was false. The Dangis believed in their witches and here was I to put them right about the world, believing as I did—in *what?*

In what? I knew no more about human beings than the Dangis. Worse, I was more confused than they. Did I understand what made my mother do the things she did? Did I understand Claude, or myself?

I was there to bring civilization to them. Had they ever dropped bombs on my parents? Had they driven Norbert out of his country and his life? True, I could persuade them to use the pills that were protecting me now against the mosquito. But those pills had been invented to stop soldiers from dropping dead of disease before they got to the appointed place for them to drop dead from bullets.

I was so agitated that I got down from the verandah, crossed the compound and walked into the jungle, an unwise thing to do. I pulled myself together, and sat for a while on a fallen tree. It seemed that I could hear Billy Green's voice (Billy, who was dead now in the war). He was saying, "Do not set yourself up." Yet that was exactly what I was doing.

5.

Shortly after that night, the Political Agent arrived on his tour of inspection that he made once a year. He was a wise Englishman whose name was Terence Creagh-Coen. We took a walk through the jungle together, in full daylight when there was no danger. I told him, in a confused manner, what I was thinking. He listened carefully. Then he said, "I suppose you'll write a book. I've often wondered—authors are such liars—I've often wondered how much money does a book *really* make?"

A week or two after he had gone, the monsoon broke. Only Dangis know how to live in the jungle under the torrential rain and the humidity. I was ordered down to the plains. Sitting with nothing to do in a Bombay hotel, I began to suppose, too, that I would write a book, and did so.

The book was called *The Prevalence of Witches.* As soon as it was accepted by a publisher, I resigned my humanitarian post with a profound sense of relief. The book was a success and therefore, as I promised, you shall hear no more about my career. I shall obey the rule I have myself laid down, with one exception. I think I should tell, for honesty's sake, how I became a Christian, without even the excuse of yellow jaundice.

6.

In this case it was euphoria. I have described how first seeing myself in print carried me over my mother's advances. Seeing my first bound book made my head swell even further. I felt that I was at peace with the world and even beginning to see some merit in its inhabitants. I was also full of forgiveness, except for a reviewer in the *New York Herald Tribune* who accused me of making the heinous mistake of confusing a lemon with a lime. I determined on a grand gesture, one befitting an author.

With the money that the book produced I went to Killarney, in Ireland, where my mother's family had lived for generations, in poverty except for occasional excursions into robbery. My mother, I need not say, was not a religious woman. But my grandmother had been devout. I decided to solve all my personal problems at a blow, and to become a Catholic.

I called on the parish priest and told him of my intention. He was an amiable and elderly Irishman. He said it was "a foine thing you're doing, a foine thing." He also said, over a glass of stout, that a lot of young men in America were going into monasteries "but they'll all be out in a couple of years," and he handed me over to the pastoral care of the assistant parish priest, a bright man of twenty-five with the firm intention, as he said, of getting out of the bog just as quick as he could. He patiently listened to all my problems, both personal and theological, for which forbearance he has been rewarded, I am happy to say, not in Heaven but right here on earth, for the last I heard of him he had landed a teaching job in Notre Dame University. He, in turn, passed me on to the Vatican.

7.

Here, in what was then called the Holy Office, I met Monsignor O'Flaherty, a very tall Irishman with a shock of white hair who was disappointed to find that although my knowledge of the Faith was sound, I did not play golf, a game to which he was much attached. I cannot say that the prospect of another writer being a convert roused any great enthusiasm in him. The Vatican was reeling, at that time, under the impact of Claire Booth Luce. I promised I would not be an enthusiastic convert, but converted I would be.

So we sat one evening on the altar steps of the empty Sistine Chapel. I talked about my life: I talked about Claude and the other Claudes I had known.

O'Flaherty waved a hand at the ceiling, which, as all the world knows, is decorated with nude pictures of Roman street boys, beloved by Michaelangelo.

"*That's* no problem at all," said O'Flaherty, "or they wouldn't be there. As long as you do no harm, and confess to the Dominicans. But—" he said, and stopped.

"But what, *monsignore?*"

"You think that the faith is going to make you good."

"Won't it?"

"No. You'll find your own way to what you are looking for. Writers do. But I want you to promise me that when you do you'll not write anything to shake the simple faith of simple people. That's all they've got to cling to."

I promised. "Besides," I said, "it is just that simple faith I want."

O'Flaherty died before the storm broke. Now, every day that I open my newspaper I find some priest trying to shake the simple faith of the simple people at the top of his voice. It is no doubt very healthy. But I did not enter the church to listen to the clamor of disputing clerics. The second Vatican Council was sitting in St. Peter's while I was sitting in my room in Piazza Farnese, finding, as O'Flaherty had foreseen, my own way.

Writers, I think, should have no religion. They should make up their plots themselves.

Chapter 9

A SHORT AND TRANQUIL

HISTORY OF SIN

1.

I would sometimes see the conciliar bishops, fifty at a time, still in their colored robes, sitting in rows in buses, being driven home to lunch. By this time I had spent many hours in the still center of my being, although as yet I could not be sure of going there when I chose. But the desire to be made good had quite passed from me.

One day I took down the missal which the assistant parish priest at Killarney had given me. It was leather bound and gilded round the edges. I had offered to pay for it but he had said that all I need do was to make a contribution to the Jesuits' Fresh Air Fund, which he in person meant to start one day, because he was sure they needed it.

I took the missal to the ancient church of San Clemente because one of the first Councils ever held took place there, under the third pope after St. Peter. I heard a mass said without opening it. I went down some steep stairs to the crypt where were the remains of the church of that early Council. I went down some even steeper stairs into the bowels of the earth and found the first church of all, so old it was not even Christian.

It was a long and narrow room, very gloomy, with the barrel vault decorated to look like the roof of a cavern. At one end was an altar, carved with the figure of a man in a peaked cap with his dagger stuck into a live bull. This was the god Mithra, and this was his sanctuary.

I sat here for a long while, so long that the Irish monk who is in charge of the place came down to see why. He peeped in, and left me to my thoughts. They were very clear thoughts. I could see right down the corridors of time, from this dank cavern, to the Christian church I had joined, to Charlotte Street and beyond, right to the day I was sitting there.

I went back to Piazza Farnese. I went to the shelves where I kept my books on theology, taking them down at random, remembering the times when I had read them and filled the margins with comments, now enthusiastic, now doubting. I sat down at the small table which was the only table in the room and served for eating and writing.

I began to write down some of the stages of that long perspective. I headed these notes with the words "A short history of sin." They are disjointed, but they are before me now and I shall try to put them together.

2.

The sense of sin probably had its origin in the East. The Brahmins had an acute and pessimistic sense of it. The Persians also had it, but they invented the useful notion of a Savior. This Savior was said to have killed a bull. A bull was therefore tethered to a high platform, and slaughtered. Its blood was allowed to trickle down between the planks. All that the sinner had to do was to stand underneath and get himself drenched by it. This disgusting rite, which would have shocked the sensibility of a cannibal, was very popular in the Roman army until the triumph of Christianity. The Savior was Mithra. The Christians abhorred the whole affair, retaining only a touch or two of it for purely literary purposes. Nobody was ever actually washed in the Blood of the Lamb.

Contemporary with Mithraism was the worship of Cybele. This arose among the Parthians, apparently one of the most relentlessly logical races in history. Here the devotee, who was suffering from a sense of sin, was required, as I have described, to cut off his testicles, one of the obvious causes of sinning.

On a higher plane, few philosophers looked deeply into the human soul. Plato had drawn an unconvincing picture of it as a chariot drawn by a good white horse and a naughty black horse, the reins being held by a sort of Eagle Scout whose duty it was to see that the naughty horse did not run away with things. This remained little more than a pretty picture until Sigmund Freud took it up and turned it into such a terrifying description of human nature that his weaker-stomached followers are now denying that he meant what he said.

The very earliest Christians felt very little sense of sin, in spite of the warnings of St. Paul, because they felt they were already washed whiter than the snow by the Savior, whom they hourly expected to return in the Second Coming. This, as we know, was delayed, a fact which seems to worry nobody but myself and some obscure theologians whose books stood on my shelves: they called it the eschatological problem, a word that only a minority of good Christians can even pronounce. But when it became clear that there was to be no instant release from the temptations of the flesh, a sense of sin began to grow. One scholar, Origen, even castrated himself, like the priests of Cybele, for which act he has rather unfeelingly been excluded from the company of Saints.

But sin was really brought back to stay by St. Augustine. He was a born writer who could scarcely have been without a pen in his hand for all his mature life, so vast was his literary output. When he was young he was a sinner, as he tells us over and over again in his *Confessions*. The only sin of his which he describes in detail is robbing an orchard with a gang of other boys. That is not usually considered a sin which should call down the wrath of God, but for Augustine it was. Clearly he thought that he was capable of being perfect, let lesser men be what they will. In the *Confessions* he is very contrite, but that was not a major work. When he came to write his masterpiece,

The City of God, things had changed. His (and our) back-slidings are due to Original Sin, a construct based on the Bible with such dialectical skill and sheer ability to write that a reader, today, has to remind himself sharply that it is not probable that Adam and Eve ever existed. Nevertheless, it was, says Augustine, Eve who brought sin into the world, and, it follows, into Augustine. His arguments are so strong that he faced his contemporaries with a clear decision: either you believed Augustine was right, or you believed that the Bible was wrong. It is no wonder that such a man rapidly rose to be a bishop.

From St. Augustine onwards, the prime sin was sex, unless it was used to produce children, God having instructed men to "increase and multiply." Indeed, the first sexual act began as a piece of feminine curiosity, but was converted into the production of Cain and Abel, a mixed result, as it has gone on being ever since. St. Augustine's thinking dominated the Catholic Church right down until the Council that was meeting down the road. It dominated Luther as well, since he was an Augustinian monk. Remove Augustine and the whole moral structure of Western civilization falls in ruins.

3.

At this point my notes broke off, for I had made yet another discovery and one which was to have a profound effect on me.

One strange passage in the Upanishads says that a

man who has found the space within the heart cannot sin. I saw that it did not mean that I would suddenly live a blameless life; nor did it mean that whatever I did would be magically right. There is a lot of rhetoric in the Upanishads, but they are never downright silly.

But I discovered the true meaning, and I did so with a sense of shock. When I stepped within the space, I stepped outside Augustine, outside the sense of sin, and beyond good and evil. These were the anguished concerns of the world beyond the space, the concerns of that writer named Menen when he went into that world. They were the ideas of other men and other places. My own true self (but this is only a metaphor) had been born before Augustine, before even his Adam and Eve and the apple.

I saw very clearly for the first time what had sent me to the Vatican and why I had joined a church. Deep within me I had sensed all this but I never had time or quiet to examine it. But it had seemed a perilous journey into the unknown. Religion had come along with its certainties and guidelines, and I had taken refuge there—a refuge from myself.

But I had spent my life not knowing that such an other-self existed. I had not even enquired if it did. This suddenly struck me as very extraordinary, and I shall explain why.

4.

St. Augustine maintained that the only way to mitigate the baseness of human nature was by the grace of

God and the safest way of making sure of this was to believe in a Savior, Jesus. There was no proof of this: it was
a matter of faith. Human nature was all wrong, then, but
faith would, or at least could, put everything right. I do
not mean to discuss this belief; what interests me is that it
satisfied the Western world through fourteen centuries.
Let us say that Christianity is the finest of religions and
one that any sensible man would adopt; or let us say that
it is a fable no thinking man could accept. The marvel
still remains that Augustine's view of human nature
stopped Western man (including me) from thinking
about *himself*. He thought about sin and salvation; he
thought about the corruption of the Church, and even
fought about it; in the eighteenth century he even made
so bold as to think that a great deal, and perhaps all, of
Christianity, was bogus. But even then he did not turn his
attention inwards to find out what his true nature was.
There were alchemists, who were mistaken scientists;
there were no mistaken psychologists at all. Men made
lists of the virtues and vices. More skeptical men, like
Hume, made lists of the passions. But nobody at all
thought of looking behind these lists to see what it was
that really made man tick. All that even the deepest
thinkers did was to find out ways in which human nature
could be improved. They knew nothing, in fact, about the
subject, except that human nature was often highly incon-
venient, and they were quite sure it could be improved.

The recipes for improvement were various. They
ranged from Augustine's Faith to Voltaire's Reason.
When Darwin proved that man was evolved from lower

animals, this was seized upon with joy as the final proof that man could be improved. Every living thing was improving. Improvement was the Law of Nature, except for some hopeless cases like dinosaurs, an exception which triumphantly proved the rule. The belief, as I shall show, is still with us, and in full force.

One man only seems to have had doubts. He was treated with contempt in his own lifetime, and scarcely much better even today. He was Schopenhauer. As he saw us, we were driven by a blind, purposeless force which he called the Will. It was something bigger than any of us, and we had no control over it. We could not influence what the Will made us do. We could only observe what we were doing. As he said, "A man *is* once and for all, and he knows in the course of his experience *what* he is."

Schopenhauer, it should be added, was one of the first men in Europe to read the Upanishads. He was deeply impressed by what he found.

5.

Thinking about this in my room I saw that all my life I had been one of the improvers. I had absorbed the opinion around me like a sponge. My "Genesis 2" had been an improving play, a plea for betterment. I had gone on to better the Dangis, and then to better my own self.

I had never stopped to examine whether all this was really any concern of mine, until now, when I saw it was not. I was free from any desire to improve anybody, and with that freedom (or so I found) a sense of guilt and sin flies out of the window.

6.

But I think I can hear some readers say:

"That is all very fine, but this man is a special case. He is an anachronism. With all his sitting among ruins, he is living in a past age. His sense of guilt and sin drove him to the Vatican. That couldn't happen to *us*. We are contemporaries. We have abolished those feelings. This is not the age of sin: it is the age of Sigmund Freud."

So it had seemed to me in Charlotte Street. But in the new-found quiet of my spirit I could see more clearly. I saw that the sense of sin had come back into the world, under a new disguise. To complete this short history of it, I shall show how that was done.

When we discussed Freud in Charlotte Street, we were, naturally, quite certain he was another of the improvers, but much more exciting, since he (as we thought) would improve sex, a thing which plainly needed it.

In fact, he was not, although many people ring their psychoanalyst's doorbell still thinking as we did. Schopenhauer saw us driven by an unresistable Will, a world view which at least had a sort of dark grandeur. Freud saw us driven by the instinct of sex, which had no grandeur of any sort. But he had more in store. From our very infancy these instincts were throttled back in the name of morality and civilization. Stunted and pruned from babyhood, we grew up to give abundantly of that fruit other men and women so desired to pick. When we were stunted enough, we were welcomed into the community of our fellows because we were at last civilized. Even more grimly, he went on to point out that we joined in this stunting of ourselves, like Chinese women of the past willingly binding their feet. Sin had never been given so terrible an aspect since the days of Dante.

Now when a man comes to a conclusion like that he usually feels that it is his duty to society to suggest a remedy. Even Schopenhauer tinkered with an argument by which he could show that people, though driven like autumn leaves by the Will, could, in a way, choose between doing the right thing and the wrong. Had anybody taken notice of him, he would probably have developed a full-scale (and respectable) morality, like Kant, whom he admired. But he was completely ignored until it was too late in his life to do any more thinking.

Freud would have none of this. Having made up his mind about human nature and the disastrous nature of our lives, he let it stand. He suggested no remedies. Indeed, he rubbed his pessimism in. He said that the repression of our instincts, the mutilation of our sexual urge, was the cause of most of the things that we admire, from painting masterpieces, to keeping the traffic running smoothly in the streets. If the repression was removed, civilization would vanish. He invented a technique by which he could discover, to some degree, what had gone on in a person during his infancy. But psychoanalysis in Freud's hands was about as inspiriting as showing a patient an X-ray photograph of his incurable cancer. It might set his mind at rest: he can go home and make his will. But it will not cure him.

Freud was a great man. We expect our great men to give us comfort, else what are they for? So Freud was misunderstood. We misunderstood him with great enthusiasm in Charlotte Street. Psychoanalysis was going to put our sexual impulses in order, and that, we felt, should be done. The people in Krafft-Ebing, with their complicated perversions, were all very interesting, but they were plainly sick. Dr. Freud would cure them. Freud himself had gone to great pains to say that he was not at all sure that he could. But we did not know that, largely because we would rather praise him than really read him. He was our savior, so we shook our sistrums and we queued up to go under the scaffold and be washed by the blood of the bull.

When his cult swept America, psychoanalysts, now making a lot of money, had to do something about it. The Americans like optimism. They will not pay for gloom. Schopenhauer sold exactly one copy of his first book; a subsequent book sold six times as many. But in America it would not even have sold that. The psychoanalysts were faced with a dilemma. They could put either Freud or the public right. They chose to change Freud, and neo-Freudism was born.

7.

The neo-Freudians announced that Freud's view of
the condition of man was altogether too gloomy. We are
not cripples who have been twisted and bent to fit into
our nooks in a monstrous society. It was a very nice society with lots of jolly people, most of whom had plenty of
money. Some people, no doubt, were not quite shipshape,
because of an unhappy childhood or some other unpleas-
ant experience. The neo-Freudians claimed to be able to
put these unfortunates right. They said they could adjust
them to the world around them, and that was their valuable place in the social structure. Long before these neo-
Freudians had come on the scene, Samuel Butler had foreseen them. He summed them up in one sarcastic word. He
called them "straighteners."

It was all a great success. I remember being asked to
contribute to a series of critical essays about the manner
and modes of the postwar world. I suggested criticizing
the neo-Freudians. The editor sharply told me that the
American public would not stand for it. The neo-Freudians were doing a great deal of good to a great number of
people. They were saving thousands from despair. The sacred bull, I gathered, had become a sacred cow.

8.

"Sin," says my notebook, *"is not sex any more. That has been coped with by the straighteners. To be sinful is not to conform."*

9.

I put the books of the psychoanalysts away on the shelves of my room, among the theologians who no longer had anything to say to me. My long days of being alone had brought their reward. I had gone beyond all this. Peeling away my life, piece by piece, like the skins of an onion, I had discovered a brute fact, a fact which the Upanishads had seized upon long centuries ago. Whenever the satisfaction of our desires involves another human being, by just so much we will be a prisoner. We shall not be ourselves. Since we are not being our true selves, we shall not, we cannot, be happy.

Thus, as I sat in my room in Piazza Farnese, it was obvious to me that the only solution to the problem of my own identity was to live, even if only for a short time, outside that framework of *us,* the others. It was not a mere question of becoming a hermit. I was that already. It was a question of thinking.

Chapter 10

WITHIN THE SPACE

1.

But the thinking was by no means easy, and on the very first day it led me into a dilemma. I was convinced that to be free I must abandon the framework of the society in which I lived. Yet, how could I? I did not gather and cook the food I ate each day. I did not make the electricity by which I read my books. I did not, in fact, even make my own bed. The wife of the janitor had insisted on doing that. Clearly, if society did these things for me, I owed a duty to society: that, at least, of keeping it going.

Nor was this a mere question of paying my bills and taxes. Twice in my lifetime the society in which I lived had gone to war. It had the right, if it were to be kept going, to ask me to go to war. The people of my own age whom I saw on my daily walk had, not so long ago, lived in a society that called itself Fascist. To keep society going they had to be called upon to believe that one single man, called Benito Mussolini, had been always right. Benito Mussolini had called upon them to go and conquer Ethiopia. A few years later they were required to say that Mussolini was pretty nearly always wrong. Admittedly, I was in the heart of Rome, and the Romans had long ago learned to turn their coats with the aplomb of the Vicar of Bray, with the addition of a few good Roman oaths that would have made the good Vicar's face red. They had done their duty to whatever society reigned at the moment. But to say that they had lived their lives as free men would be absurd.

It was clear to me, then, that my duty to society is a very mixed affair that might change completely with the times. It could not therefore be a *moral* duty, for if the word "moral" had any meaning at all, it meant that there was a fixed code which one should obey. It seemed to me, as I sat in my room, that no such thing existed.

2.

But this statement was so extreme that I thought I should examine it with the greatest care, even if it took me days to do it. I searched for something which all men would agree should always be done whatever the circumstances.

I took up the proposition that one should obey the law, provided the law had been made with the free consent of the members of the society in which one lived. This was easily disposed of. With the free consent of the British public a homosexual, if discovered, could be sent to jail for a number of years. Even while I sat thinking, with the free consent of the British public a law was made saying he could do as he pleased provided he was an adult and his partner consented. By the light of the electricity I did not make I took down a book by a fellow writer describing how he had been arrested and sent to jail amid the greatest humiliation for doing something which he was perfectly free to do before the book had time to get into a paperback edition.

It might be thought that his situation was an exception, but it is not. I have seen a great number of people in the same plight.

A little while ago I traveled widely in the Deep South of America, from the Carolinas to the Mississippi. When I returned to New York, my friends expected me to be shocked at the state of the Negroes. It was, indeed, deplorable. But what struck me even more was the state of the whites: good, honest American citizens who entertained me hospitably in spite of my color. For generations these good people had done their duty by society, which had previously consisted in keeping the Negro down as a second-class citizen. The law had raised no objection. Now it did. Most of them were still prepared to obey it. But if they did not face the situation with a Roman obscenity, it was only because Southern manners forbade it in the presence of a guest. They were, after all, in the position of those people whom I met on my daily walk to the Piazza Navona.

I thought more deeply. "Love your neighbor" (the thing I had so notably failed to do) seemed a duty which was above politics, above changes in the law, above swings in prejudice. But to love your neighbor you must at least share some of his habits and opinions, though not all. I think a Sadducee would have found it fairly easy to love a Pharisee. Though there were points in which they differed, they had even more in common. Some of my neighbors in Piazza Farnese had once gone out in black uniforms, seized people of liberal opinions, poured castor oil down their throats and then beat them into insensibility. To say that I could love such people is, I suppose, possible, but it would be in the way that Jesus loved the money-changers, whom he drove from the temple with a whip. Nor do I think they would have wanted to be loved by such as me: as an ostentatious liberal, I would have been due for my dose of castor oil.

In whatever way, then, I regarded my duties to society, and on any level that I took them, it involved me in the vicissitudes of the people I lived among. Nor would those changes be my own doing. I would have to follow. I would be a prisoner of my fellow men.

3.

But I was a prisoner who had been given a ticket of leave. For a while I had been free: I had seen my life, my parents, my friends and my enemies as though none of them was a part of me. The moment had come and gone, but who was this neutral person, this tranquil surveyor? What was this self I had discovered?

A strange uneasiness came over me. I felt that, at the

last moment, I was going to miss the truth by making some mistake, by taking the wrong road. I turned back to the Upanishads, but suddenly I found them confused and tantalizing. I read and re-read a page which had puzzled me and still could make no sense of it. I tore it out and pinned it to the wall. The page said that even in our dreams we were not free. Dream-people could still chase us, beat us, revile us and upbraid us for our shortcomings.

This, I saw, was true. The world followed me into my bed and clutched at me more than it did when I was awake. But, said the page on the wall, there was still another self—the one that existed while we were in a deep and dreamless slumber. This was the real self.

It was an enigma. An unconscious self, to me, seemed to have no meaning. Yet I was sure that in the enigma was the answer to my uneasiness that I was missing the road. I remember that I thought about it one long evening until, round about midnight, I fell into just such a sleep as the page described.

4.

In the small hours I suddenly awoke and saw with great clarity that the enigma was not a puzzle at all. It was a warning.

I had, indeed, nearly missed the truth, and it was due to vanity. All along I had been assuming, without really knowing it, that the self that I was seeking would be a rather superior affair, better than the average run of selves. It would have its own judgements, its own opinions of other people's selves, and its opinions would be right. Naturally this superior self would want to be free to go its own enlightened way.

I remembered the Olympians who lived across the way from Charlotte Street, gracefully dispensing tea in Bloomsbury. They too considered themselves superior. How could they think otherwise? They were more cultured than most, more reasonable than most, more humanitarian than most, and more open-minded than almost anybody. Did not unknown and dubious youngsters come to tea? Did not D. H. Lawrence come to cocktails and denounce them on their own hearth rugs? They even had an ethic of their own, or rather one they had adopted. It was by a philosopher called G. E. Moore who, with great brilliance of argument, had set up a code by which to live. It closely resembled the way the Olympians lived in any case, which showed how right it was.

I laughed at the Olympians when I was in Charlotte Street. I laughed at them again in the middle of the Roman night, but most of all I laughed at myself. I saw I was tarred with the same brush.

Our true self is not superior to other people; it is not inferior either. It is not touched by other people at all. It does not wish other people to be better, or to be worse; it neither punishes nor praises. It can be totally indifferent to the world, as if sleeping; or it can awake and observe, but with the same indifference.

"Not that, not that," say the Upanishads, in the puzzling phrase which has echoed down the centuries. Now I saw its meaning. *I* was not that; nor anything that you could name in the world around me. I was not good, or bad; I was not a son, or a friend, or an uncle, or a cousin. I was not a success, or a failure. I was not even a middle-aged man in a room in Piazza Farnese seeking to answer a Pope. *I* was perfectly free of all such things because I had always been free. The world had not made me. It had merely thought it had.

I got up, put on a shirt and trousers and sandals, and I went out of my three doors into the great square with its two fountains. The night was cool and calm. I sat on a stone bench and felt a great peace descend on my spirit. I was a free man for the first time in my life.

5.

But next morning I had to get up, shave and walk to Piazza Navona for my coffee. The world may not have made me, but I had to go out into it and pretend that it had done so. The Upanishads promised me that there would be no difficulty, and there was none. When I had found myself, they said, I could go back into the world "and enjoy women and chariots," whenever I pleased.

So I went back into the world, that splendid Roman morning, and I enjoyed it—the people in the square, the morning sun on the fountain, the newspapers with their news of war and violent deaths—but all in a different way, and that way has remained with me ever since.

I cannot describe the feeling, because it lies too deep

within the person that I now am. I can only give a parallel.

Imagine that among the group of Dangis who sat round my acetylene lamp in the jungle was one who doubted the witches and their works. He knew nothing of the anopheles mosquito, and never would know. He had no better explanation of the young man's death than the others. Witches, however, did not move him as they moved others. If it came to voting whether a witch should be bribed or beaten, he would vote, as was his duty. But he would not raise his voice, *he would not push his fellow men about.* He would suspect that they were showing a great deal of emotion without knowing what they were talking about. He would leave it at that.

The man who has found the space within the heart is like one who sits in a theatre watching the rehearsal of a play. Suddenly the director calls upon him to take one of the parts. He goes onto the stage, he takes his script, he reads the lines as best he can. He goes back to his seat, as calm as when he left it.

6.

It was at this point that Piero knocked at my door, with his mocking gift of bananas and his real need to be helped. He was the first person I had talked to at any length for three months, but I found it no effort. I told him, as I have described, what I had discovered, and he, in his fashion, discovered himself.

But talking to him roused a doubt in my mind. Could this thing be done? Could one live for any length of time in the world with the feeling that I now had? I had been alone a great deal. Was it perhaps a hallucination born of loneliness? I have known a similar sense of release while riding a camel deep into the Sahara Desert. But that was no discovery of the Self. It was forgetfulness. I remembered nothing of the world until returning, I saw the domes of the oasis rising behind the distant dunes. Could one live the life of a spectator without being a hermit?

It was a question which troubled me until, one day, Piero gave me the answer.

He did not go off to his tropical isle to live the life of a new Gauguin. Instead he received a brown and ill-printed postcard warning him to prepare to do his duty under the draft. He was very angry. He said it was preposterous to train him to be a soldier. If one thing was certain it was that Italy would never fight another war. He tore up the card. Then came a second card, to his house, calling him to arms. He went because, as he wisely said, his mother already had trouble enough. A second member of the family in prison would be monotonous.

He went to a remote camp in the south of the peninsula to do his basic training. Then he wrote me asking if I would come to the ceremony of swearing-in the recruits, "at which point," he wrote, "I become a real soldier (*they* think)."

I went south. I stood among a crowd of relatives and parents and watched the troops march and countermarch.

I searched their faces under their round helmets but I could not see Piero. There was an interminable religious service, but I still could not see him. The troops flung their right hands in the air, swore to defend their country and dispersed. Still there was no Piero.

I walked slowly to the gate amid the departing parents, thinking that he had fallen ill. I wondered whether a mere civilian would be allowed to see him. Then I heard a voice behind me.

"Om! Master of Wisdom, I bring thee offerings."

I turned and saw him, almost invisible under his helmet, but smiling his ironic smile, as ever.

We embraced in the Italian manner.

"And where are the offerings?" I asked.

"Ah," he said. "Yes. No 'bananas this time. Bullets." He fished into one of the innumerable pockets of his uniform and brought out a clip of spent ammunition.

"It's the first they allowed me to fire, and damned near the last, too. They're saving ammunition. It costs the Americans too much."

I thanked him. We went outside to a bar.

"What's it like?" I asked him.

"Ridiculous. But it's done me no harm." He drank off his glass, ordered another and told me the usual stories of boot camp—corporals, sergeants, a day and night in the guardhouse.

After a while he suddenly said, "Have I changed?"

"Not in the least."

"Good. I didn't mean to. You know, it's exactly like you said. I'm play-acting. Salute! Attention! Dismiss! Yes-

sir, nosir. Sorry, sir. That's how they like it, and that's
how I do it. Except once, and then they sent me to the
cells. Now I'm a good soldier. Why break their funny little hearts? So I play along until I get to bed in the evening. Then I read some of the books you gave me, and
I'm still myself. It's a trick worth knowing. Thanks."

7.

So, Gottlieb, I at last found out what it was all about,
and I could tell the Pope, if he had time to listen. All
those things in the boxes you have will throw little light
on it. They are like suits of armor in a museum: they tell
you nothing about the man who wore them. But my
search was finished. It was time to leave my room.

8.

I moved. I took a normal apartment outside the walls
of Rome. I began to write letters and to answer the telephone. But for a month or two I was convalescent. Not in
my body; there I had never in my life been so well. But
my spirit had changed. Now that I knew that the world
could never eat me, it seemed a very pleasant place. But I
did not have much to say to it. My friends were welcome
company, but only for a while. I would grow restless with
them, and wish to be alone.

I began to wonder whether I would ever play a normal part in society again. I began to doubt whether I would ever take on the responsibilities of living with other people, even though I was triple-armored against any assaults they made on me. I hoped I would not have to put it to the test.

9.

It was now July. A letter arrived from a boy, taking me up on a promise. His name was Graham. He was fourteen, blond, blue-eyed and English in his looks, and full of intelligence. After my mother's funeral I had gone down into the country to talk to the boys in a private school owned by an old friend of mine—an English custom among writers, artists, actors and anybody who has done something that the boys might be thinking of doing when they grow up.

Graham was the ward of my headmaster friend. He had been the ward of various people since he was three. But he was not an orphan. His parents were alive and willing to pay for his education; but they did not want him in the family home. They gave no reason. There was a younger sister, much loved by them, and perhaps there lay the trouble. There was nothing in Graham's character that could account for it, nor did they ever say there was. He was a fine boy, but utterly bewildered.

This was the story that my old friend told me. I met Graham. He was polite. He showed me his collection of matchboxes. Then he told me he wanted to come to

Rome. He had read a book of mine about the city and I saw that it meant something to him beyond its beauty and deeper than its history. It was Camelot; it was Atlantis. I promised he could come for a holiday when his school term finished.

He arrived, still a puzzled and lost boy, but determined that Rome would be what he dreamed it would be. He rode over the problems of a strange language, a strange food and the lack of companions. Not that he lacked friends for long. The Romans, so indifferent to foreigners, took to him immediately. Soon, wonderful to say, they were treating him as one of themselves, one, moreover, of their own vast families. He sat at their tables, he joined in their baptisms, their weddings and their *festas*.

One day he talked to me about that different world, back in England.

"I never knew *why*," he said. "Why did I have no family? What had I *done*? It was all right, really. I mean, school was fun. It was the holidays. I remember one Christmas. I was staying with the Robinsons, a nice family. They liked me. I thought I was going to spend Christmas Day at home. But late on Christmas Eve there was a change of plan. They didn't want me at home. I had to stay on with the Robinsons. I was wondering a bit about if I would get any presents from my mother and father, but that turned out all right. My father drove by and left a package for me. We opened them all—the presents, I mean—next morning at breakfast. Mine were okay. But everybody was jumping up and thanking everybody else and saying, 'It's *just* what I wanted.' I couldn't thank anybody. I just sat there, looking at my presents. I have never felt so miserable in my life."

I asked him how old he was when this had happened. "Twelve," he said.

10.

The time came for him to go back. But he asked me if he could stay, stay to live in Rome, stay and live with me.

I asked him why and he said because he felt sane.

I consulted Piero, who, too, had liked him and who had christened him, with affection, the Happening.

"The Happening wants to stay. For good," I said.

"Why not?"

"Why *not?* I'm a middle-aged man who's never married and never had children. And he's a teenager in *this* day and age. And I shall have to be responsible for him and everything he does. I won't even know how to begin."

"You could begin," said Piero, "by telling him that all that about his family doesn't matter. It's just a part he played in a play. It doesn't affect him. You know. Like you said to me."

11.

So he stayed. He is eighteen now, tall and impressive in his manner, and self-assured. So far from being a problem, Roman mothers turn to him for advice about their wayward teenagers. He gives it, and in turn takes photographs of them for a book he has been commissioned to do on the people of Italy.

He has been back to his family. His father proudly took him round the town to show him off to his friends. It was, after all, just a play, with a plot full of misunderstandings, as plots are, and which has come out all right in the end.

The counsel of the Upanishads has worked—out in the wide world and not only in my room in Piazza Farnese.

If it had not, I would never have published this book.

Chapter 11

HOW IT IS DONE

1.

I have so far spoken of my own experience. I must now treat of other persons who may wish to experiment with the technique. I shall risk repeating myself but I may gain in clarity.

In the first place the system is not confined to any one age or sex. The seekers after their true selves in the Upanishads include women, and even a boy, about whom a whole Upanishad has been written. Anybody, then, can try it, but one thing is essential at the very beginning. The seeker must be urgent. He must have a deep sense that he is being smothered by people alien to him; that he is being drawn hither and thither without stop; that he cannot say "I think this" and be sure that it is really he who thinks it. The situation is familiar—a wife bedeviled by a marriage, a husband sunk without trace in his family life, a young lover aware of being too much in love, a student trying to think for himself amid the clatter of his companions and the unceasing bray of his instructors.

Familiar, but not often intense; yet if anyone is to submit himself to the long rigors of lonely self-analysis, and carry through to the end, then that feeling must be so deep as to amount to a malady. It often comes with a crisis—a death, a failure, the break-up of an affair or the end of a marriage, or the few days of clarity that come when one has recovered from a serious illness.

Then is the time to go off alone. You cannot find yourself amid other people. You merely find *them*. The seeker cannot discuss what he is doing with others, not, at least, while he is doing it. They will tell him what they think; he listens, and in no time at all he is back on the treadmill.

But there are many ways of being alone. My room was little more than a cell, but it was in a piazza of stupendous beauty. In the same way someone who likes forests might choose a hut in one, or a sailor a lonely cottage by the sea. Loneliness need not be harsh; there is no need to be an anchorite. In fact one must be very careful not to choose a hostile environment. Crossing a desert begins quite well for meditation, but it is remarkable how soon you arrive at the point when nothing is in your head but the desire to get to the other side. The surroundings can be agreeable, though not so much as to intrude. On the other hand, nothing whatever can be achieved by lying alone on a beach in the sun. There is nothing supine in the system. It is hard work; perhaps the hardest work one has ever done in one's life.

The next thing to do is to reduce the routine of living to its simplest terms, or, better still, to have no routine at all. Everyone has his private anchor to the world:

in my case it was the sumptuous and regular Roman meal. As I have said, this has to go. Vanities of dress and appearance must be abandoned, along with letters, telephone calls, newspapers and the like. Nor should too many people know what you are doing. Some must. Tell them not to seek you out. But others will, if you are not too far away. They will come, thinking that your seclusion will have made you as sweet and saintly as a cloistered nun. Swear at them: it is the only thing to do; and the more vulgar your language, the more enduring will be its effect. When you have found the space within the heart, it is another matter. Then, nobody can take it away from you.

You are going to examine your life to see how much of it is really yours. But one's memory cannot be relied upon. It is well to surround yourself with mementos, hooks on which to hang your enquiry. You are not on holiday; you have not gone to get away from it all. You have gone away to see through it. Books, photographs, letters, keepsakes are all useful. Your walls should grow to resemble those of a retired actress, except that beside your triumphs you are careful to put reminders of your disasters. I regretted having sent off so many of mine to Gottlieb, but packing the box had been a spur to me, and I had others in Rome.

The actual process of examining one's own life in loneliness and in utter impartiality must be experienced to be really known. But it can be approached in a simile. When a marriage breaks up that has lasted many years, each of the partners spends many hours rehearsing in his or her mind what has happened. Old quarrels are reviewed, old delights resavoured; puzzling incidents that were never explained are puzzled over once again.

The examination one undertakes alone is a little like that, but with one vital difference. The partners of a broken marriage do not stand outside themselves. They are sunk in the emotion of love or hate, anger or belated tenderness. The lonely seeker after himself must check these sharply. He is not a novelist. Flaubert, when he had written a scene about somebody weeping, would rise from his writing desk with tears running down his cheeks. The seeker must be no more moved than a judge on the bench listening to evidence which sounds tragic but may be a clever lie.

The partners of a broken marriage do not make notes. They may write long and heated letters to each other but they do not put their thoughts down on a card index. The seeker should and must. He will have his own methods. I, as a writer, kept a notebook. But again, as a writer, I was careful not to shape my notes into polished phrases and thus falsify them. I deliberately wrote ugly and ungrammatical sentences. I misspelled. I used symbols instead of words. I would say that for another person a tape recorder would be better, but I have a great dislike of the sound of my own voice, so it would not do for me.

After some days the seeker will have a number of the skins of the onion he is unpeeling safely in his notebook or on his machine. Let us call these his Public Selves. He should now go over these repeatedly, like a student revising for an examination. The step which follows is as strange as the division of the fertilized egg cell that I wrote about in my first play.

Let us go back to the student. He is in the examina-

tion hall. The question paper is put on his desk. He reads
it and panics. The question is (let us say): "Describe the
foreign policy of Henry VIII." He doesn't know; he has
never studied it. All he can remember is that Henry had
six—or was it eight?—wives. He scribbles "six/eight" on
a sheet of paper. Then he writes "divorce." Then "Pope
against it," and there, in a flash, he has the whole trend
and nature of Henry VIII's foreign policy.

The seeker does not even have to make these jottings.
As he reads or listens to his Public Selves a Private Self is
born from them. This Private Self is utterly unconcerned
with winning good opinions from schoolmasters, lovers,
wives, husbands, friends or anybody at all. It has all the
arrogance of the inspired creative artist way ahead of his
times and not giving a damn for the public. It has all the
certainty of the scientist who has made a discovery that
has set the cat among the pigeons and who says, "Yes, but
I *know* that this is true."

This Private Self is an inspiriting thing to discover
but there are two things to be carefully observed about it.
The first is that there is a serious danger—a *very* serious
danger—on the way there.

It might happen that when the seeker has laid out
all his Public Selves in order, his meditations are inter-
rupted. The result is disastrous. The man from Porlock
broke off Coleridge's dream by knocking at the door, and
"Kublai Khan" was never finished. Just so, the whole
labor of the seeker can be lost and he can be left in a
worse state than when he began.

It is easy to see why. If the seeker has been honest
with his survey of his Public Selves, he will now see him-

self as the pawn of others' design, a leaf driven in the wind, a poor thing without any constant mind of his own. If he stops at this point and goes out into the world he will do so with all his confidence destroyed; nor will he find it again for a long time. If the man from Porlock turns up, the only thing to do is to kick him out of the door before he has time to open his mouth. Above all, *stay in your room.*

If that is done, the Private Self will emerge, and all is well. The seeker can break off his meditation if he has to, and go back among his friends and enemies without fear. He will have all the confidence he wishes, and perhaps too much to be thought a good fellow by his companions.

But (and this is the second point) the Private Self is not the space within the heart.

At this point the seeker should take still firmer measures with himself. He should eat and drink a bare minimum. He should not fast, because fasting draws back his attention to his body, and his aim now is to forget it. He must eliminate all the small things that add to his bodily comfort—the hot bath, the comfortable armchair, the too comfortable bed. Above all he should fight down the demand to take exercise, to go out into the world and stretch his legs. He should lie relaxed in his room, and stay there.

It will be filled with ghosts. My own, at this stage, reminded me strongly of a frontispiece of an old edition of the works of Charles Dickens. Dickens sat at his desk, and all around him floated the tiny figures of his famous characters. His skill as a novelist would, I fancy, reduce them to order. Just so, one has one's Private Self to marshal and judge the company, and this the seeker should do.

But soon—if he *stays* in his room and has no contact with the world—this gradually seems to be a mere game. The characters begin to bore, and they fade. The seeker's past lives, the skins of the onion he has peeled away, grow thin and meaningless. Remembered passions wilt and seem a waste of time; old battles seem to have been over nothing. The Private Self struggles to go on commanding and arranging, but it tires, like a director in some theatre who has realized the play will be a failure.

Then one hears a call. It comes from somewhere deep in the mind—the word "heart" is a metaphor. It calls one away from the Public Self and the Private Self. It is like a voice on an island, calling across the sea.

Now you must be still, quite still. You must die a little death.

Then a great tranquillity steals over you. It trickles like water through the cells of your mind, washing them clean. You think of nothing, nothing at all, but with a crystalline awareness, and it is the end of your search.

2.

What is it? I do not know and I believe I cannot know. To *know* one must have all the tools of logic, induction, observation and all the rest. But I had been deprived of all of these. I had reversed Descartes. He said "I think, therefore I am." But I *was,* I existed, calmly, quietly, without a care in the world; yet there was no thinking.

I can only say that the space within the heart seems to be some core of consciousness which has been overlaid by all the necessities of living, and it may be the core which sustains us against all the changes and chances we must suffer from the day of our birth, and even before. Most of us do manage to hold together some personality of our own, battered and twisted by others as it may be. Some unfortunates do not, and we lock them away in asylums. Is it because this tranquil, unchanging and unchangeable core dies in them?

3.

The seeker, who is no longer one, can now leave his room. He can go back into the world and take up his life again—his work, his family, his friends and his enemies. He will notice that he sees what is going on around him with a new clarity and above all, a new calm. He may lose his temper, but—and I found this strange—instead of deepening his passion as he proceeds, he instantly sees himself (his Public Self) losing his temper, and he is tranquil so quickly that he has to conceal it a little, in order not to appear odd in his behavior. It is the same with all the other feelings—love, sexual desire, hate and all the long list of our turbulences. They come and go, but much more mildly, being observed.

As for his past lives, these, too, no longer trouble

him. If art is emotion recollected in tranquillity, then he surveys them with the calm eye of an artist. He has no need to defend himself, and the urge to blame others is gone. Above all, he sees with great simplicity that other people have much the same problems as he, problems that can only be solved by leaving them, as he had done.

The space will remain with him. Even in the company of others, he has only to will himself back through his Public Self, back through his Private Self, and he is once more at peace.

And why not? He has discovered who we really are. He has that peace which passes the understanding, but in which everything is understood.

APPENDIX

The Upanishads are difficult, even for Hindus. For the Western reader they can be daunting. There are a great number of them, and the majority throw very little light on the discovery of the self. I used two of them—the *Brhadaranyaka* and the *Chandogya,* but at first reading they can be as hard and strange as their names. I have therefore thought it best to write this note, which goes some way to explain their background.

Let me return for a moment to J. Maynard Keynes. If anyone were to ask us if we knew the value of money we would all reply that we certainly did. Yet, of course, the truth is that we certainly don't. The value of money is fixed, virtually every week, by our governments, who, in turn, do as the financial experts tell them. The decision of these people can be so inept that they can plunge the world into bankruptcy, as they did in the Depression. We do not mind. We do not call for their heads; we do not even know what heads to call for. We accept their decisions as meekly as a child accepts his father's order that he must henceforth have less pocket money until things get better. If someone tells us that we should not be crucified on a cross of gold, we reply that Pontius Pilate knows best. Thus when I talked to Keynes I did not talk about money because I knew nothing whatever about it. I left it to him.

That is the way we live now, and only a few people suspect that it might be an exceedingly silly way. The ancient Hindus did exactly the same thing, and were quite content. The value of money was not the problem; theirs was not a money economy. The problem was the value of everything else, and this they left to the Brahmins: that is, to their priests.

Now a priest, from the earliest shamans to the reigning Pope, is essentially a person who tells us how to please the gods. If we ask him how he knows, he replies that questions like that are a sure way of making certain that the gods are not pleased at all. But in these words, the argument seems ridiculous. Put in another way, it can seem like one of the most impressive constructs of the human mind. St. Thomas Aquinas, for instance, in his *Summa Theologica* does not prove that the Catholic faith is right. He begins with the assumption that it is: then, in a shelf of volumes, he goes on to draw the consequences. That the shelf is a mass of gibberish to a Moslem does not prevent St. Thomas from being one of the most influential thinkers who ever lived.

In the same way the Brahmins assumed that they knew how to please the gods and drew up a great body of work showing how it was to be done. They completed a vast number of prayer incantations and rituals with which, they said, the gods could be brought to heel. There is no reason to assume they were charlatans. Famine, epidemics, and sudden death are not the daily lot of mankind. Life in an agricultural society usually runs placidly. The Brahmins could take all the credit for the happiness of their followers, and when things went wrong, that was all grist to the mill as well. Clearly, some necessary prayers had not been paid for or a sacrifice not done. What financial expert has ever come forward and said that inflation was *his* fault? It is always ours. We are spending too much. Our pocket money must be stopped.

With that parallel in mind, we may perhaps look upon the ancient Hindu with sympathy. He believed the Brahmin when the priest said he could run the gods, and he therefore thought that the Brahmin ran the world, including himself. He therefore willingly paid the Brahmin to say or do the right thing on his behalf whenever he did anything at all. There were prayers and sacrifices to be made when the Hindu rose from his bed, when he returned home to have sex with his wife, and when children were born to him, when relatives died, when he embarked on a new enterprise, when he went on a journey, when he safely returned, when he fought his enemies, or made merry with his friends. Grace, we might put it, was not only said at mealtimes. It was said over everything in the daily round; and it was always said by a Brahmin who was the only one who knew the right words for the occasion.

The Brahmins, for their own convenience, gathered the prayers and the rituals into missals and prayer books, which were at first committed to memory, and later written down. These are the Vedas, not to be confused in any way with *Vedanta,* though outside India they almost invariably are.

But the Brahmins were not to have it all their own way. Some six centuries B.C. in India (the period I have been discussing) there was a tiny minority which began to feel that the whole system of their civilization—its laws, its customs, its beliefs—was hollow and fake. In our times such people would tend to come together and set up a reforming group of some nature or at least write letters to the newspapers. The doubters and the troubled ones in India were more drastic. They turned their backs on their fellow men and went off to some remote place to think. In the same way, when life in the declining Roman Empire began to stink to high heaven of falsity and corruptness, some determined Christians went off into the Egyptian desert to live alone in caves.

It is perhaps unfortunate that the best known of these Indian rebels is Gautama Buddha. There can be no doubt that he did discover a way of escaping from the code of civilization, for he was a man with a powerful intellect. But he was also a member of the minor royalty of the time, and it would seem that *noblesse oblige* caused him to return to his fellow men and to instruct them. He was a gifted speaker and, like similar platform performers, was not unwilling to simplify things to suit the mental level of his audience. He summed up the way to escape in what he called the Eightfold Path. You had to observe right views, right intention, right speech, right action, right livelihood, right effort, right mindfulness, and right concentration. This advice has attracted millions of sincere people ever since, but it unfortunately has a great resemblance to the advice of a good and kindly maiden aunt.

But there were others who perceived the same line of thinking as Buddha but pushed it further—so far that they arrived at a discovery that they saw shattered every conception that men had of their relations with their fellow men. The discovery put nothing in its place—no new theory, no eightfold paths of good behavior—only total rebellion and total peace of mind. This discovery was the space within the heart.

The thoughts of these rebels against organized society have come down to us in a series of short books. They were called the Upanishads because they were not books at all. The title means "sit down beside me," or, in other words, "the only way you can learn what I have to say is to come here and listen." That was simply because reading and writing had not yet been invented. It is a pity that there are some people who can never be satisfied with a simple explanation, because they have romantically assumed that Upanishads mean that the doctrine is secret. That is bunkum. The Upanishads tell, over and over again, of a stream of people who came and sat down beside the rebels, who were perfectly willing to instruct them, provided they paid the fee. The fee itself is clearly laid down. They must bring fuel to keep the rebels' cooking fire going and offerings of food to put in the pot. If they were young they had also to act as the philosopher's general domestic help. The course took several years. There is even the description of an entrance examination; one aspirant pupil charmingly admits that he does not know his father's name because his mother didn't. The philosopher compliments the boy on telling the truth and admits him to the course without further ado. The final proof that the rebels had no intention of keeping their teachings secret is that they willingly instructed women.

Since the Upanishads were not written down, they had to be memorized, and this has led to their principal difficulty. The original teaching must have been straightforward, otherwise nobody would have troubled to listen. But when this came to be handed down by word of mouth (and maybe this process lasted for generations) it was cut up into an easily memorized catechism, made up of formulas which were constantly repeated, with the new information tacked on to them in small bits. The same thing happened with the poems of Homer. Everybody knows that for him the dawn was almost always rosy-fingered and the sea wine-dark. It has been calculated that there are twenty-five of these formulas, or fragments of formulas, in the first twenty-five lines of the *Iliad* alone.

But, for all that, the teachings of the rebels were so impressive that in due time they were written down. As I have already pointed out, in spite of the fact that they contradicted the Vedas, by some chance they got bound up with them. Centuries passed, and some keen brains noticed the conflict. They set about reconciling the two. The task, as it may be imagined, was a large one. It resulted in an entirely new philosophy which was neither to be found in the Vedas or the Upanishads. Six whole schools of Hindu philosophy arose, one of which was the Vedanta, with which, in this book, I am not concerned at all. In this process the text of the Upanishads was often distorted and sometimes downright faked. But a sort of awe for ancient wisdom made the commentators and the copyists leave in enough of the original teaching for it to come through, with study and thought.

The Western reader has a wide variety of translations to choose from in several languages. The translators are often very gifted, but when they come to the word *atman* most of them fall flat on their faces. They call it "the soul," which it is not. The reader should be more wary. He is much in the position of Adam when he named the animals in the Garden of Eden. To call a tiger a "tiger" Adam had first to see the beast. So it is with the *atman*. You cannot really know what it is until you have found it, and that can only be done by going off alone and looking for it. Once you have found it, you really do not care what it is called, because it is so much your own private business.

However, a distinguished Indian and scholar, S. Radhakrishnan, faced up to the problem. He dismissed out of hand the word "soul." Instead he chose the word "self." It was the best that could be done, and that is why the Western reader, whatever the translation he is reading, should keep Radhakrishnan's *The Principal Upanishads* beside him for checking. Parts of Radhakrishnan's English translation are eminently readable, parts not. The Western reader should begin with the seventh section of the eighth chapter of the Chandogya Upanishad.

Then he should shut himself alone in some quiet place, and think.

ABOUT THE AUTHOR

Aubrey Menen is one of today's most distinguished writers. He has written countless magazine pieces and over a dozen books, some of which include *The Prevalence of Witches, Rome for Ourselves, Speaking the Language Like a Native,* and *A Conspiracy of Women.* Presently settled in Rome, where he wrote *The Space Within the Heart,* Mr. Menen is at work on a new novel and on a collection of travel pieces.